THE
ENCYCLOPEDIA
OF
SIGNS
AND
SYMBOLS

THE
ENCYCLOPEDIA
OF
SIGNS
AND
SYMBOLS

JOHN LAING and DAVID WIRE

STUDIO EDITIONS
LONDON

Publisher's Note
The Publishers have made every effort to identify copyright holders and to obtain their
permission but would be glad to hear of any inadvertent errors or omissions.

This edition published 1993 by Studio Editions Ltd.
Princess House, 50 Eastcastle Street,
London W1N 7AP, England.

Reprinted 1994

Printed and bound in the Slovak Republic

ISBN 1 85170 967 3

Contents

Introduction 6

Early Recordings 8

Ancient Worlds 16

Africa 52

The Americas 76

The Pacific 132

China 142

Eastern Philosophies 152

Japan 166

Islam 192

Societies and Belief 220

The Celtic World 258

The Medieval World 274

Heraldry 284

Towards the 20th Century 298

Introduction

A story is told of a Chinese Emperor who summoned his court painter and demanded of him that he make a painting of a fish for the Royal Appartments. The painter reassured his lord as to his loyalty and left to undertake his task.

Days passed; then weeks. The Emperor sent a messenger to the painter's studio to find out what was happening. The messenger returned with the report that the painting was not ready.

Months came and departed. Every envoy to the painter was curtly dismissed with the same information; that the painting was not yet complete.

After a year had passed, the Emperor could contain his impatience no longer and stormed off to the painter's studio himself. The painter is sitting there, quietly and evidently quite at ease. The Emperor is furious, 'Where is my painting?' he shouts. At this the painter bows silently, draws a large sheet of paper towards him, sets a variety of colours in jars before him, picks up a large brush and, within two minutes, has executed the most wonderfully sinuous image of a resplendent fish luxuriating in limpid waters.

The Emperor can scarcely control his rage, 'If it is so easy, why have I had to wait so long?' Still maintaining his silence the painter goes to the back of his studio where there is a large alcove with doors reaching from the floor to the ceiling. He opens the doors and out onto the floor pour thousands of paintings of fish . . .

Looking at the visual motifs contained in this book it is easy to take for granted the extraordinary range of visual imagination that they represent. They sit on the page with an easy naturalness, as though things had always been that way. But, of course, they represent a residue left, over many thousands of years, by legions of people, most of whose names will never be known.

The technique of the presentation of these images has been kept deliberately simple, to the point of starkness in most cases, so that the elemental and shared themes in these pieces can emerge, uncluttered by incidental particularities of colour, texture or line.

Certainly one of the components in the forcefulness of these images is their very anonymity. Much of the recent history of western culture, in particular, (and by recent we mean virtually all of the last thousand years) has been preoccupied with the emergence and development of individual consciousness. Individual consciousness in Western societies tends to be associated only with certain, given human beings and, by the nature of things, these self-standing people have names by which they can be identified. Now, not only does a name label a person for everyday purposes, but this name also acts as a landmark across time. Landmarks can be very helpful, as we all know. But it has become an odd characteristic of our culture that people concentrate on the landmark and fail to observe the deeper identity that it is there to signify.

Cultural history in the West is studded with names; schools; -isms. It is difficult for us to appreciate work unless it has a name tag attached to it from which we can take guidance; if there is no name, we are uncertain (how strange it is that a painting, supposedly, shall we say, by Rembrandt, should be so valuable until it is revealed that it is not by the master but by an assistant; at which point it becomes virtually valueless!). The 'name' becomes synonymous with the 'work' and, consequently, we end up seeing only the name and scarcely a trace of the heart of the work at all.

Yet, the vast majority of the images in this book do have undeniable power, despite the fact that we can attach no names to the people who made them. What gives them this strength is the aspect that we overlook when we remain fascinated only by a name or a reputation; their universality.

The book is organized along roughly chronological and geographical lines. It is difficult to classify this material in an absolutely watertight way: various chapters overlap eachother with the kind of imagery they present; a chapter concerned with older human societies is found to overlap with other chapters dealing specifically with work produced in Africa, the Americas or the Far East.

There is an unavoidable inevitability to this, which is more reassuring than it is disconcerting. The themes touched upon by the unrecorded people whose images appear in this book have strongly uniform threads interconnecting them. These links prevail despite distances apart of many thousands of miles or separations in time by an equally large number of years. This is a property of human culture and experience that was perceived by, amongst others, Joseph Campbell and made the subject of books of his such as 'The Hero with a Thousand Faces' and 'The Masks of God'.

This book begins, and indeed aims, only to graze the surface of a pool of human experience the boundaries of which can never be fully known. The vast majority of the images presented here are each but marker flags which can lead the curious into rich and mysterious worlds of belief or enchantment, fear or wonder. Readers of this volume, interested in the mysteries hinted at in these elusive images, might well turn later to Campbell for a much deeper exploration of a subject which, no matter how much we might think of it and how deeply we might study it, has no end.

John Laing

This page
The Lily. As recorded in Amarna Knossos, Ialysos and Korakou.

The images on these pages and on the following six are facsimiles of drawings compiled by Sir Flinders Petrie who lived from 1853 to 1942.

He was a leading figure in the establishment of archaeology as an accurate historical yardstick of the progression of human cultures.

The drawings lack any significant artistic finesse. But they do represent the record of a man who could bring a clear and uncomplicated eye to the traces of

different societies which, although they might appear strange at first sight, are just reflections of normal, everyday, human experience. Many of the images

in the rest of this book have been amassed in succession to this man's pioneering survey of ancient and distant worlds.

This page
More images of the lily from Egypt and from the Greek world.

This page
The Octopus.
A richly rewarding
shape duly explored
in the Greek world,
Spain and,
immediately above,
in China.

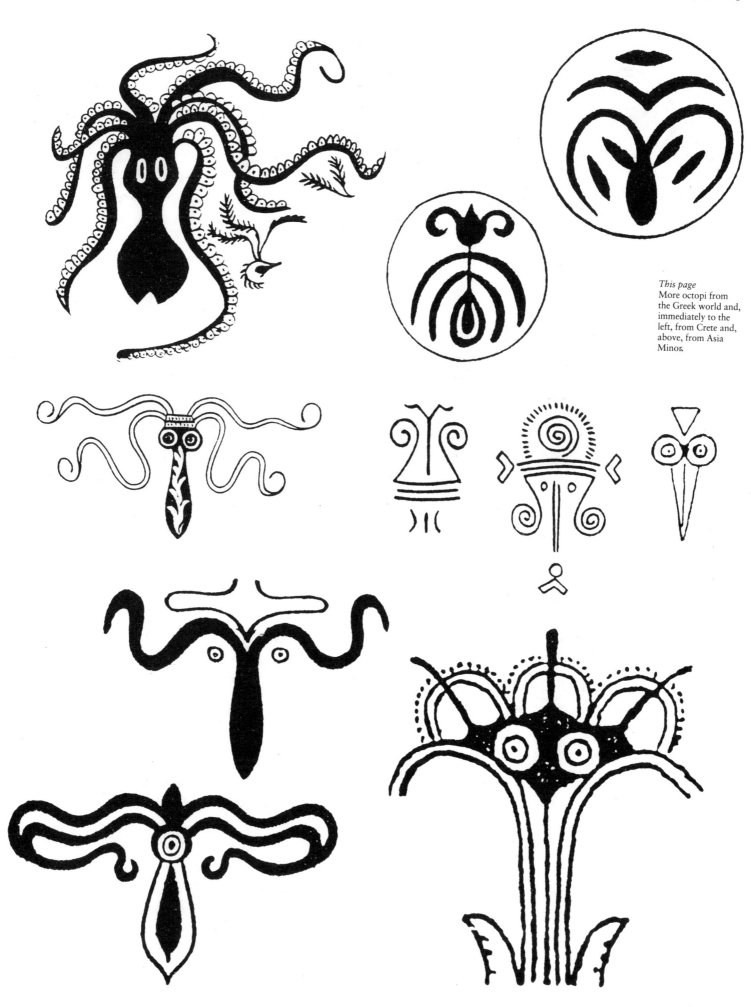

This page
More octopi from the Greek world and, immediately to the left, from Crete and, above, from Asia Minor.

11

This page
The nautilus and two sea urchins from the Eastern Mediterranean and Europe.

This page
The nautilus and the
squid as recorded in
the Eastern
Mediterranean.

13

This spread
The spiral, frequently found in nature and a constant object of fascination for human decorators. The examples on these pages come from Russia, through Scandinavia into Northern Europe thence into the Mediterranean world, Troy, Egypt and Asia Minor.

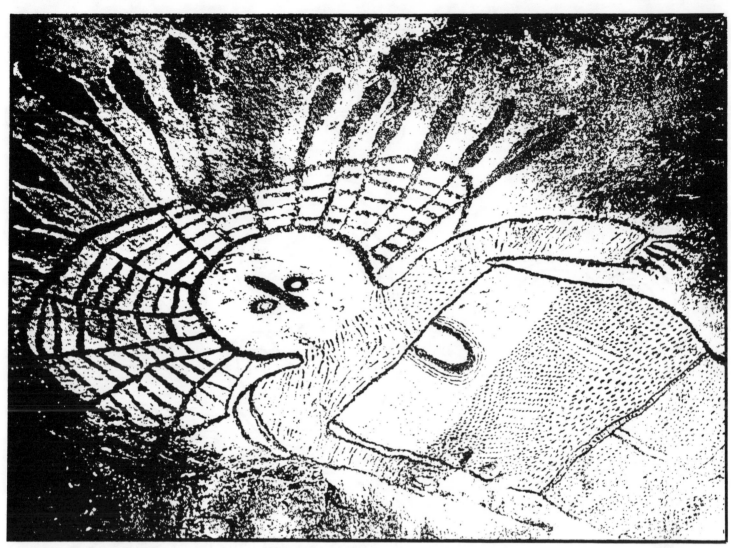

Top
Cave painting from
Kimberley in Western
Australia.

Above
Dancers.

Left and left above
Various figures from
wall-paintings.

Above
Man with
boomerang.

Left
Wall painting.

Above
Man with forked
spear.

This spread
Rock engraving and painting from Sweden and Southern Africa.

Opposite page
Rock engravings
from a cave on the
island of Götland.

This page
Rock paintings from
Spain and Southern
Africa.

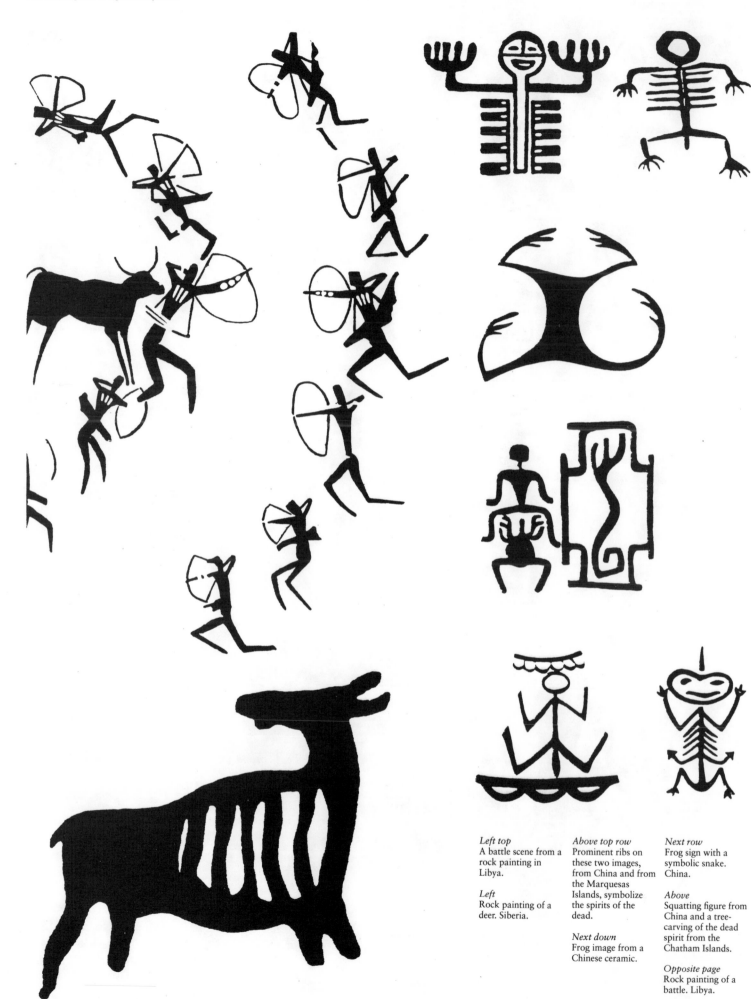

Left top
A battle scene from a rock painting in Libya.

Left
Rock painting of a deer. Siberia.

Above top row
Prominent ribs on these two images, from China and from the Marquesas Islands, symbolize the spirits of the dead.

Next down
Frog image from a Chinese ceramic.

Next row
Frog sign with a symbolic snake. China.

Above
Squatting figure from China and a tree-carving of the dead spirit from the Chatham Islands.

Opposite page
Rock painting of a battle. Libya.

Left
Inuit drawing of a
god with huge teeth.

Right
Inuit animal
painting.

Left
Inuit spirit.

Right
A composite animal.

Left
Two spirits in
trouble.

Right
The mother source of
animals that live in
the sea.

Left
A spirit who helps those who have broken tribal laws.

Right
Drawing of a shaman playing a drum.

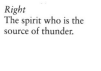

Right
The spirit who is the source of thunder.

Above
Drum painting of a shaman with energy rays piercing his head.

Left
A helping spirit.

Right
A portrait of a shaman by himself.

This spirit was drawn by an Inuit after meeting it. It is a spirit of comfort but has such a disturbing appearance that the human it visited ran away in fear.

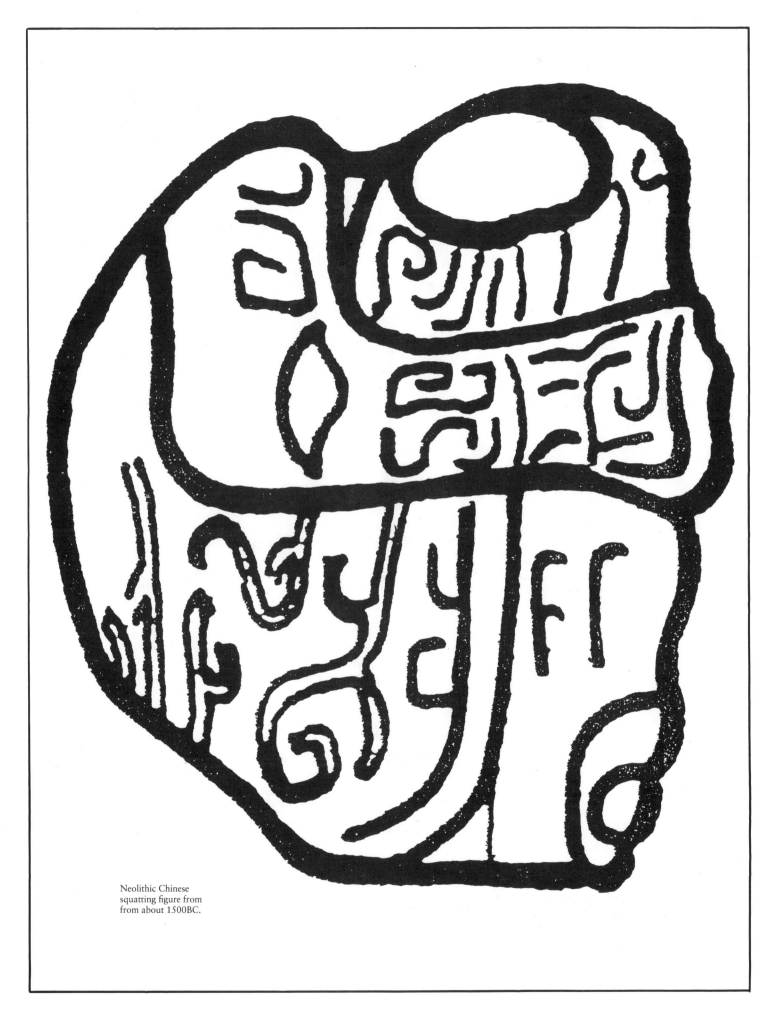

Neolithic Chinese
squatting figure from
from about 1500BC.

Above
Pictographs of the Shang Dynasty, China. From left to right: bull, ram, boar, stag, cow, ewe, sory. All from the 2nd Millenium BC.

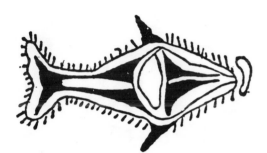

Left
British Columbian Indian drawing of a wolf swallowing a human being.

Left above
Drawing of a fish from New Ireland.

Left middle
Eskimo drawing of a whale.

Above
Rock engravings from the Atlas Mountains.

Left
A kangaroo hunt.

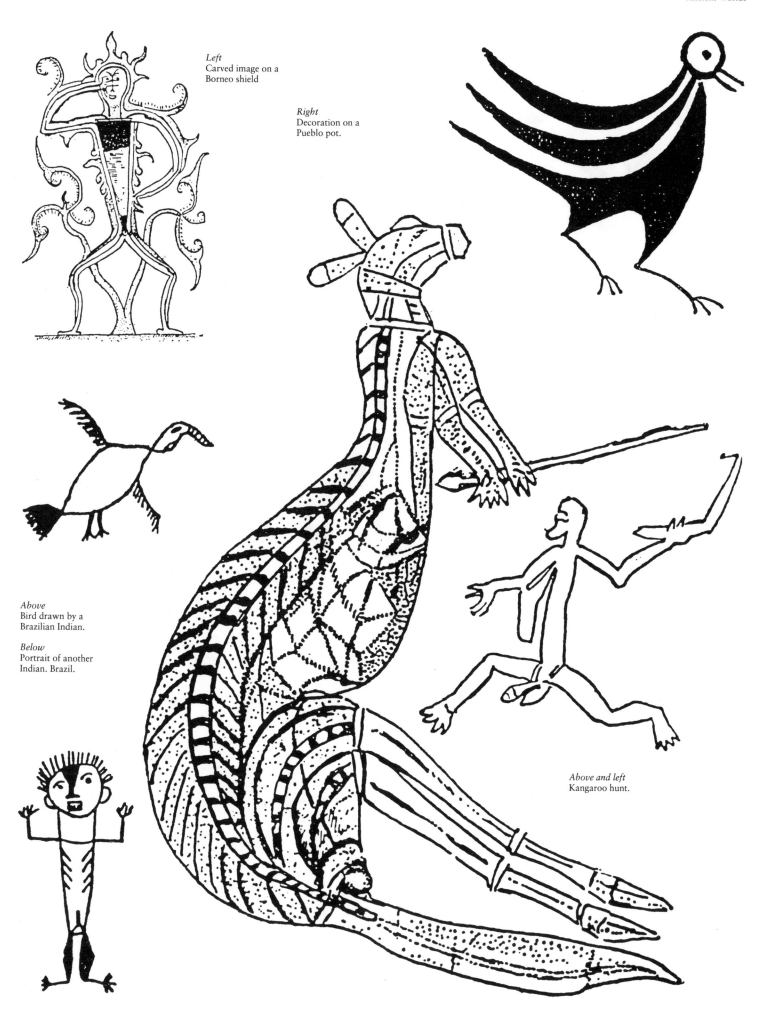

Left
Carved image on a
Borneo shield

Right
Decoration on a
Pueblo pot.

Above
Bird drawn by a
Brazilian Indian.

Below
Portrait of another
Indian. Brazil.

Above and left
Kangaroo hunt.

29

Below
The revealed ribs of
this figure indicate
that it is the image of
a dead ancestor. New
Hebrides.

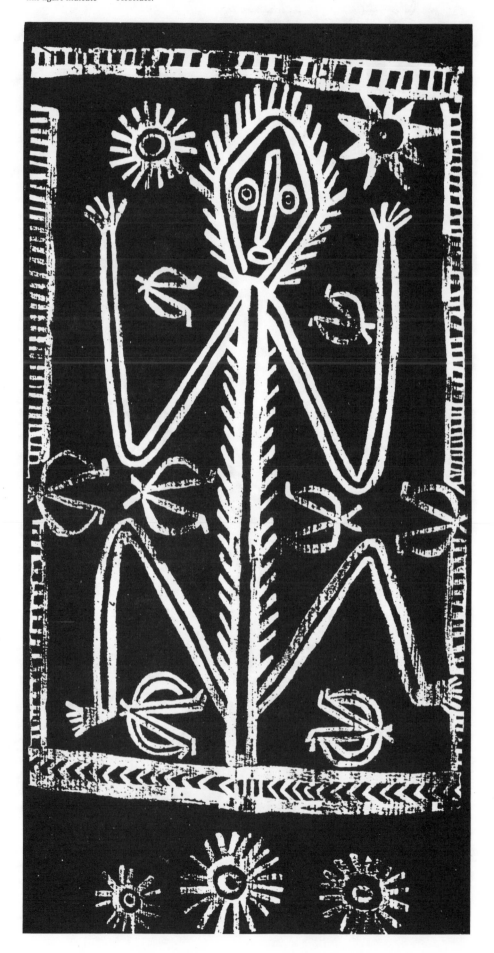

Top
Wooden carving.
Papua, New Guinea.

Above
Etruscan vase
decoration.

Below left
Spear decoration.
New Guinea.

Above
Peruvian textile.

Below right
Motifs from the
Admiralty islands.

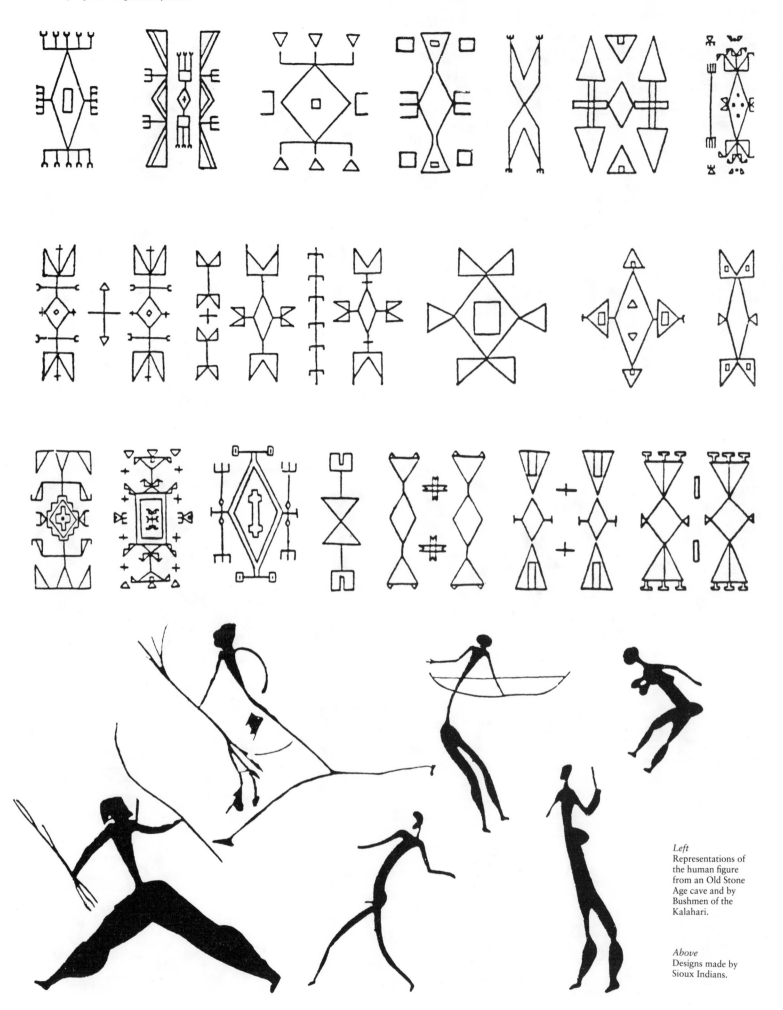

Left
Representations of
the human figure
from an Old Stone
Age cave and by
Bushmen of the
Kalahari.

Above
Designs made by
Sioux Indians.

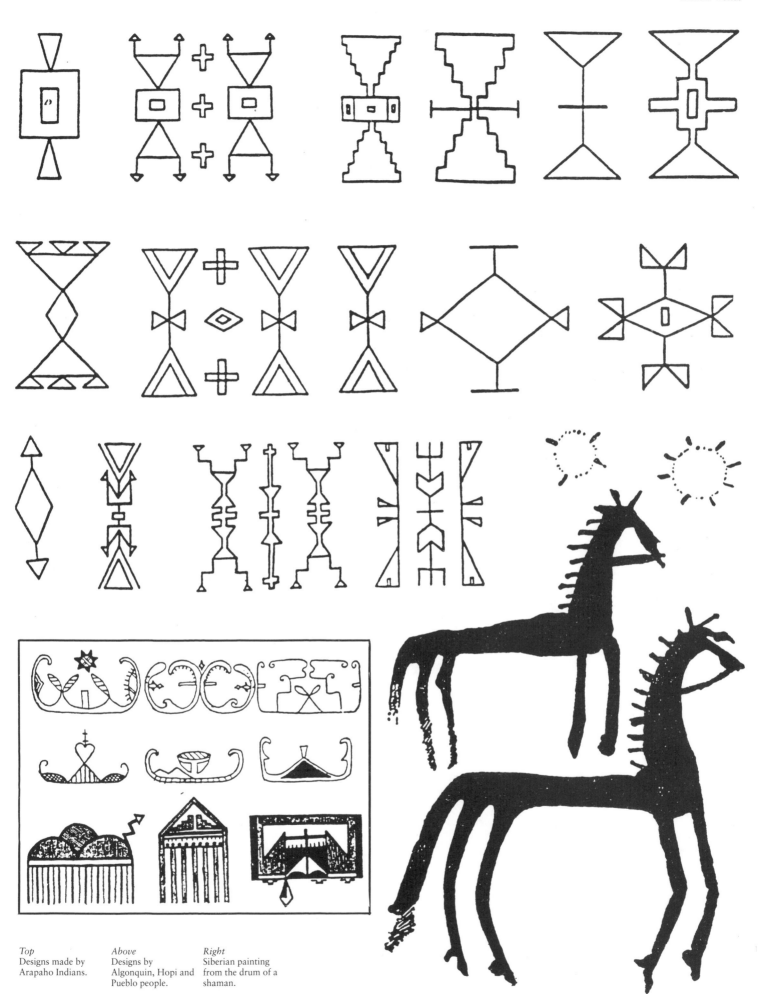

Top
Designs made by
Arapaho Indians.

Above
Designs by
Algonquin, Hopi and
Pueblo people.

Right
Siberian painting
from the drum of a
shaman.

Top left
Ruandan designs
denoting various
artefacts in daily use.

Left
Design on a dried
animal hide.
Shoshone Indian.

Above
Bushongo patterns.

Left
Haida tattooes of a
duck (left), raven
(above) and a shark
(above right).

Top
Kwakiutl painting of
a raven.

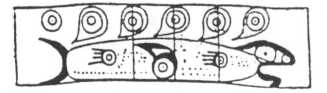

Top
Kwakiutl painting of a killer whale.

Above
Pieces used in a gambling game. British Columbia.

Right
Haida deign for a dish containing a representation of a shark.

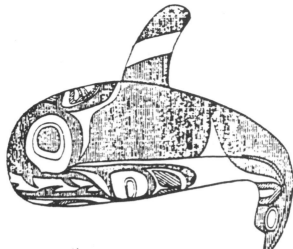

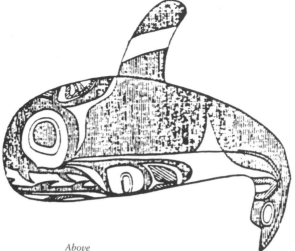

Above
From a Haida
carving of a whale.

Above
Frigate bird motif.

Left
Decorated shells with
various
representations of a
snake.

Right
Haida painting of a
bear.

Above
Haida tattoo of the
moon.

Below
Carving of a frigate
bird.

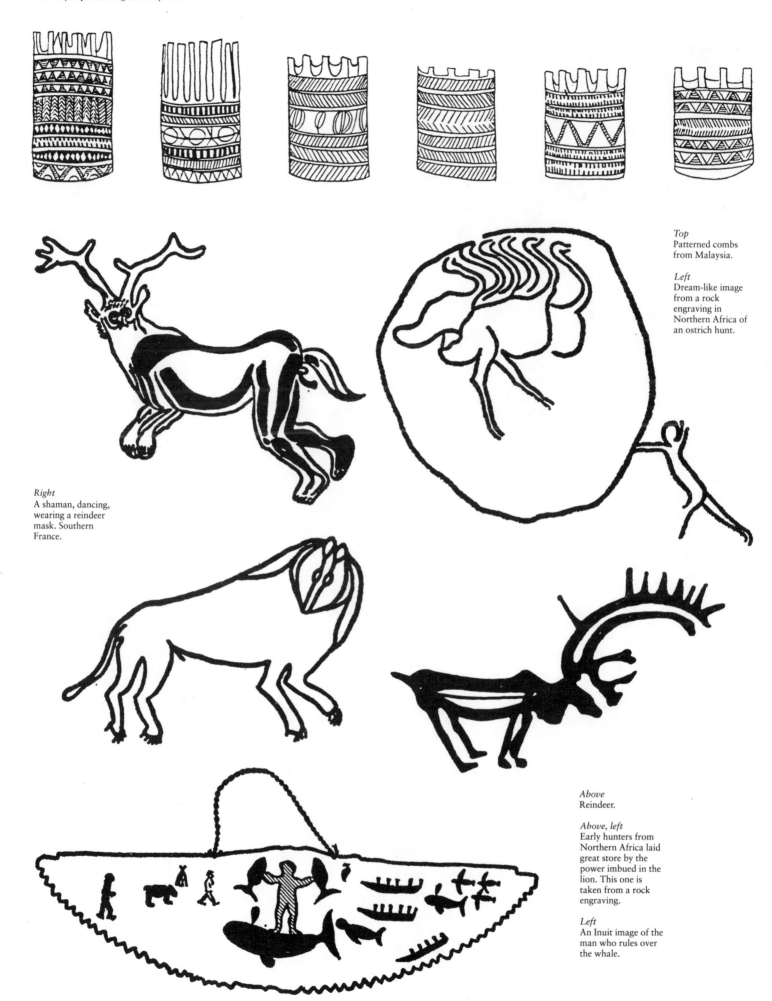

Top
Patterned combs from Malaysia.

Left
Dream-like image from a rock engraving in Northern Africa of an ostrich hunt.

Right
A shaman, dancing, wearing a reindeer mask. Southern France.

Above
Reindeer.

Above, left
Early hunters from Northern Africa laid great store by the power imbued in the lion. This one is taken from a rock engraving.

Left
An Inuit image of the man who rules over the whale.

Right
Australian spirit.

Left
Inuit drawing of a
seal and a serpent
with two heads.

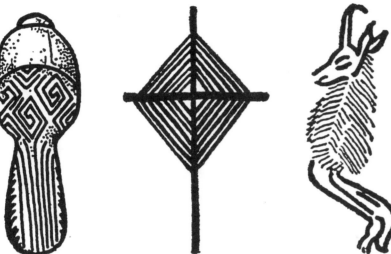

Far left
Symbolic female
figure found in the
Ukraine.

Centre left
A cross with woven
interconnects.
Australia.

Near left
Dancers with
antelope masks.
The Dordogne area
of central France.

Below
Pueblo Indian pot
decoration. The
arrowed line
represents the lifeline
of the animal.

Above
A rock engraving of
a deer from Siberia.

Above left and right
A decorated altar for
making sacrifices.
Lapland.

Above
The Goddess of the
Animal World.
Greece.

Above
Reindeer with
shaman wearing a
wolf's head mask
and beating a drum.
Russia.

Right
Deer with life line.

Right
Deer drawn in X-ray
style. Norway.

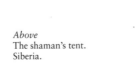

Above
The shaman's tent.
Siberia.

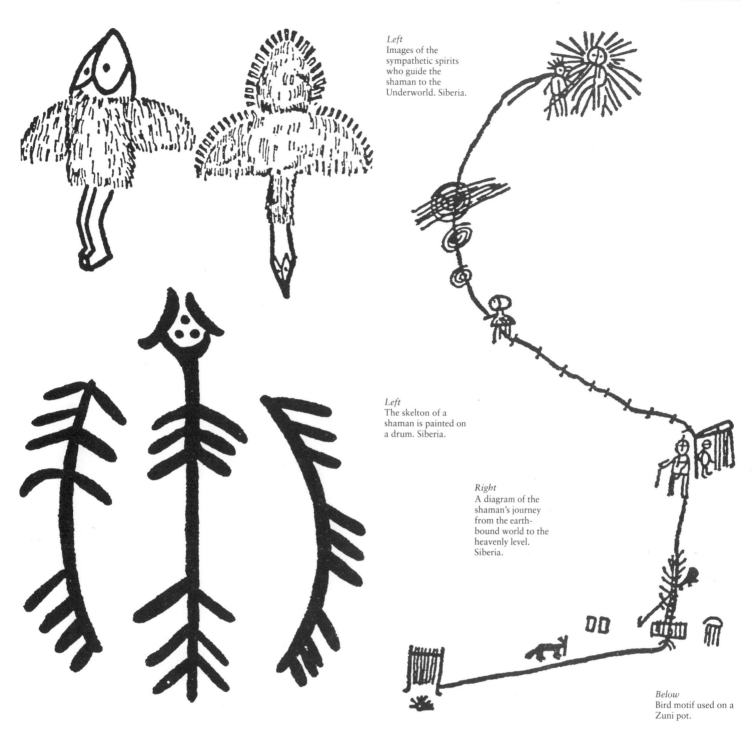

Left
Images of the sympathetic spirits who guide the shaman to the Underworld. Siberia.

Left
The skelton of a shaman is painted on a drum. Siberia.

Right
A diagram of the shaman's journey from the earth-bound world to the heavenly level. Siberia.

Below
Bird motif used on a Zuni pot.

This spread
Decoration on
Pueblo pottery and
from Mimbres, New
Mexico.

Top left
Shawl woven from
llama wool. Peru.

Left
Siberian bear spirit.

Top, coming down
A New Guinea
wallaby; a horse
from the Chou
period in China;
Aboriginal bark

painting of a
kangaroo; wild-cat
from Peru.

Above
Animal motifs on an
Indonesian fabric.

Top and far left
Details from a
woollen carpet
woven in Iran but
found in Siberia.

Left
Peruvian figure.

Above
Peruvian god with
jaguars.

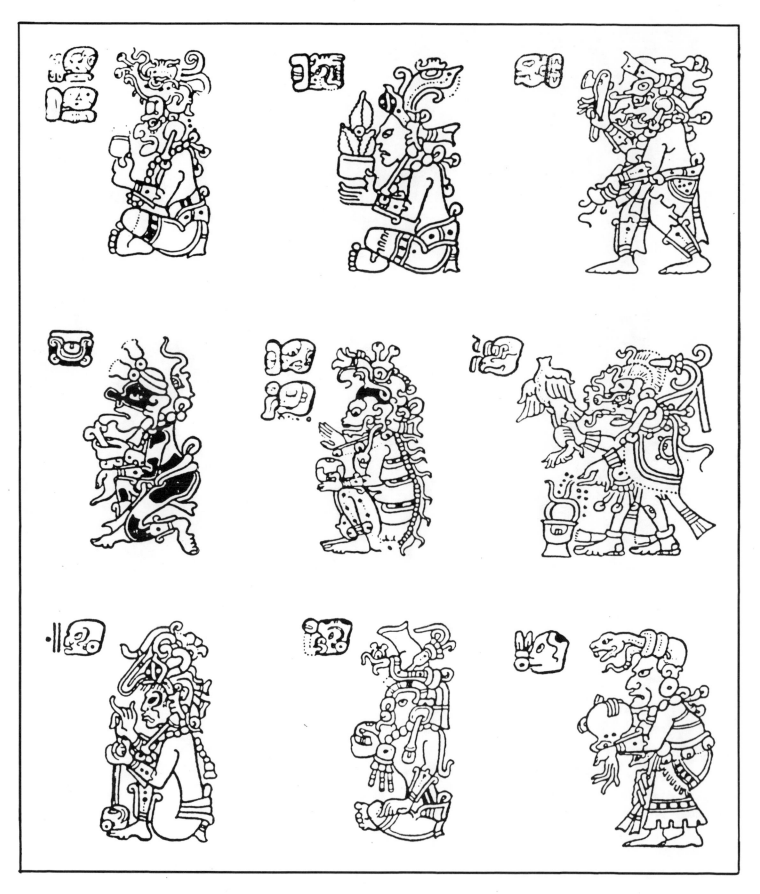

Above
The Mayan religion possessed many gods. Illustrated here are the most important. Left to right, top down: The chief god, Itzamna; the corn god; the rain god. the war god; the death god; the wind god, the god of sacrificial death; the goddess of birth and weaving; the god of the North Star.

Above
Phillipine fabric
decoration.

Above and left
Warriors with the
severed heads of
conquered enemies.
To capture the head
was to possess the
spiritual power of
the vanquished.

Left
Carved stone relief
from Peru.

Above
An engraved figure,
on a vase, wearing
the jaguar mask.

Top
Figure on a Peruvian
textile.

Left
Mythical figures on Peruvian fabric.

Above
Woven fabric showing a jaguar's head with two other jaguars on either side.
Peru.

Above
Pictographs drawn by Dakota Indians

Right
Fishing motif from Nootka Indian head-dress.

Left
An embroidered figure on a Peruvian cloak.

Left below
Embroidered figure from the Huichol Indians in Mexico.

Right and below
Decorations from a Mexican tablet.

This page
From a Mexican
painting.

Left
Woven textile. Ibo,
Nigeria.

Right
Nalindele mask from
Zambia.

Below
Weights used for
measuring gold dust.
Ashanti, Ghana.

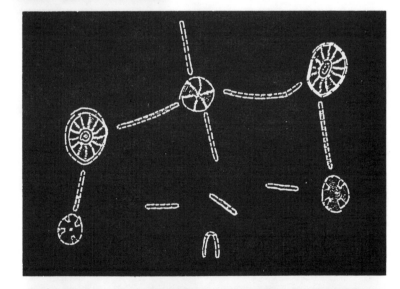

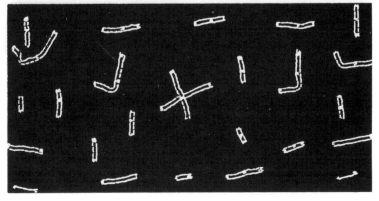

Above
Execution of Yoruba
king.

Right above
The ship of King
Agadja of Dahomey.

Right below
Symbol of the lion of
King Glele.

Far right above
Cloth decorated with
beads. Southern
Africa.

Far right below
Decorated fabric
from South Africa.

Above
Appliqué figures
from Dahomey.

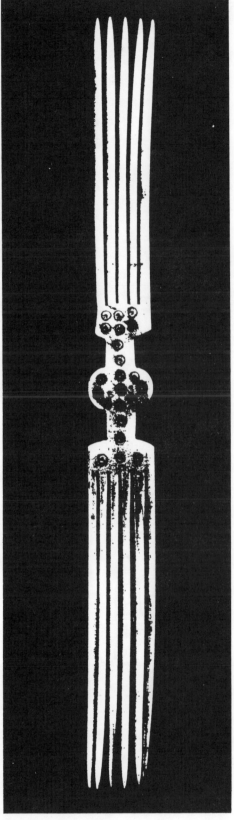

Above
A comb carved in
bone. Zulu.

Below
Symbolic signs from
the Ivory Coast.

Left hand column -
top down:
Possibility of
correcting mistakes;
Home as a place of
safety;
The all-seeing eye of
the King;
The desire for peace;
Life everlasting.

Right hand column -
top down:
God as the star of
heaven;
Faithfulness;
Patience and
endurance;
Forgiveness;
The eternal
connection between
life and death.

Right
Combs of bound-up
slivers of hard wood.
Zaire.

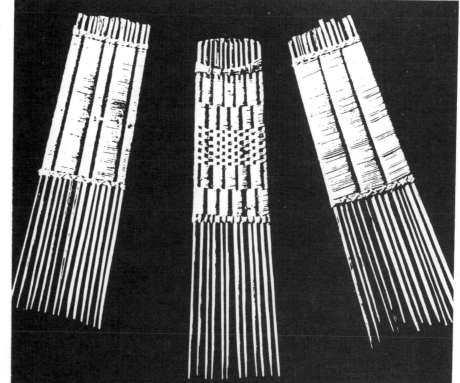

Above
Symbol of two
crocodiles joined
together. West Africa.

Left
Hairpins from
Angola.

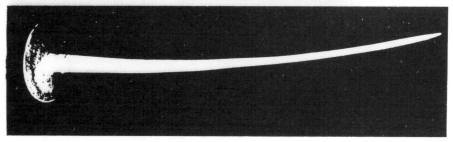

55

Above
Detail of patterns
used by the Yoruba
people in Nigeria on
resist-dyed fabrics.

Below
Tie/Dye cloth from
Ghana.

Bottom
Resist-dyed cloth
from Cameroon.

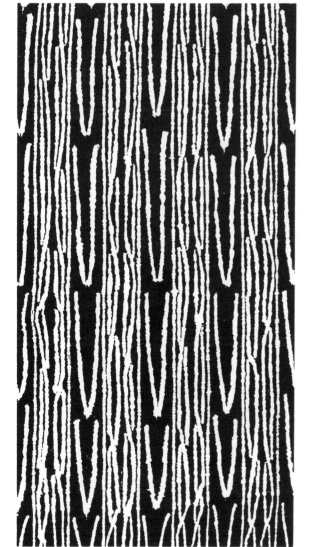

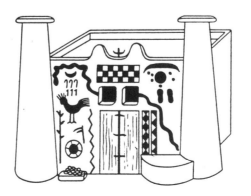

Left
Diagram of a Dogon
temple with symbolic
bird and snake signs.

Above
Appliqué cloth from
Dahomey illustrating
the history of the
country from its
beginnings in the
17th Century.

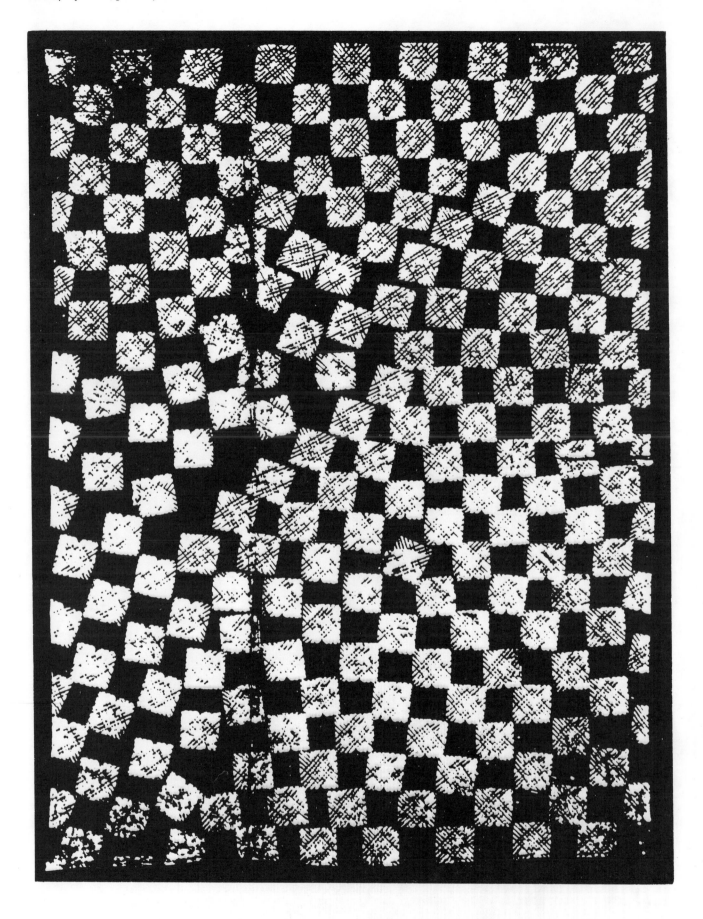

Above
Resist-dyed cloth
from the Ivory Coast.

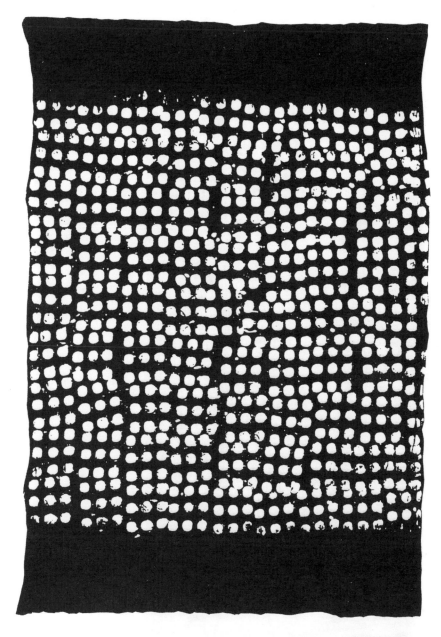

Above
Woven fabric.
Liberia.

Below
Yoruba fabric.

Above
Resist print from the
Ivory Coast.

Right
Detail of fabric at far
right showing
sophisticated
brocade weaving by
the Yoruba in
Nigeria.

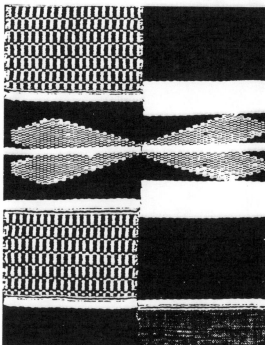

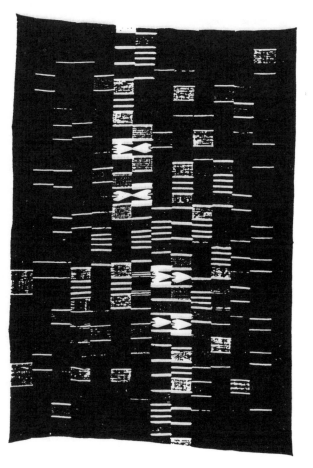

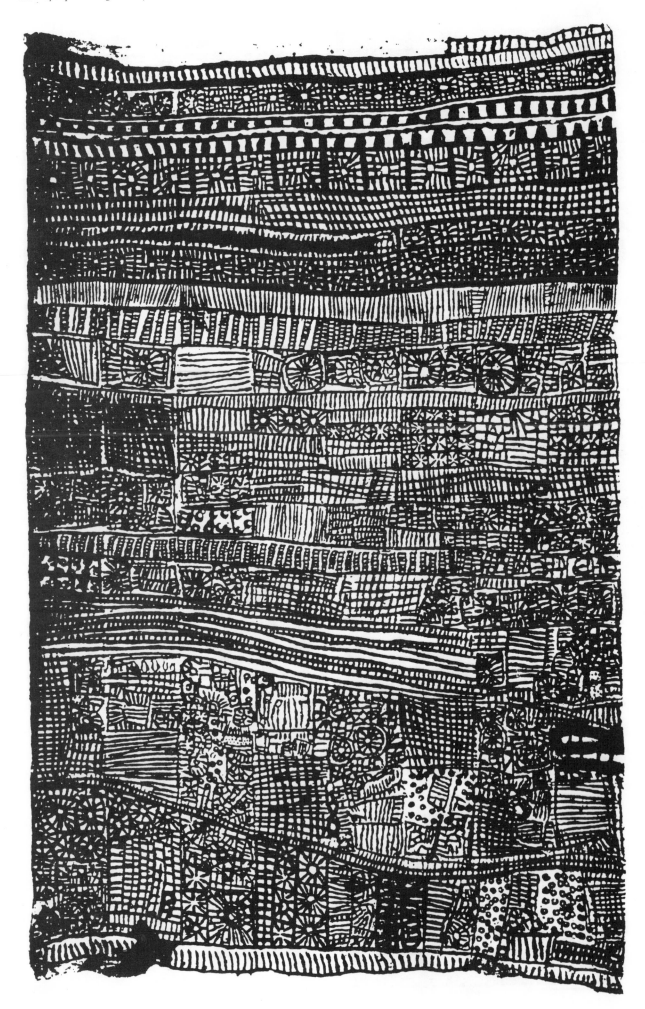

Left
Painted cloth from
Mali.

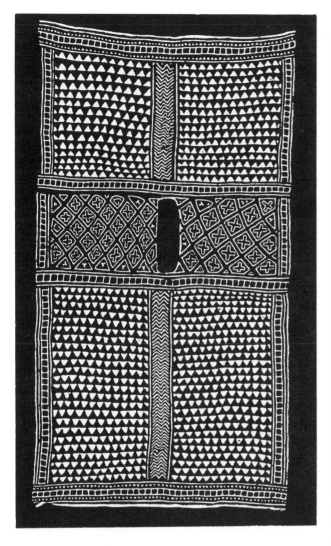

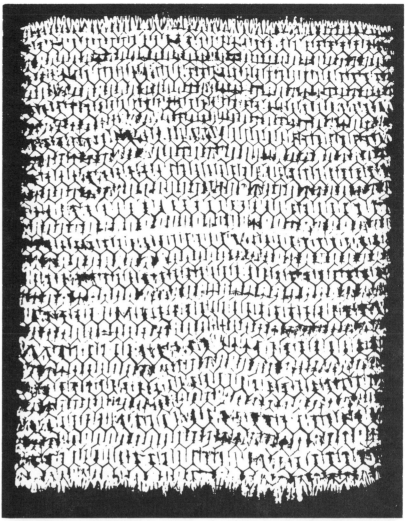

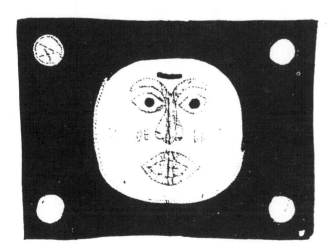

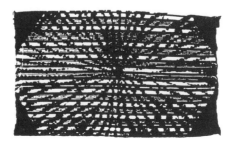

Top
Painted fabric for
clothing. Mali.

Above
Appliquéd cushion
cover depicting the
Sun. Dahomey.

Left
Tie/Dye cloth from
Sierra Leone.

Top
Tie/Dye cloth from
Sierra Leone.

Above
Appliquéd regal
tunic from Ghana.

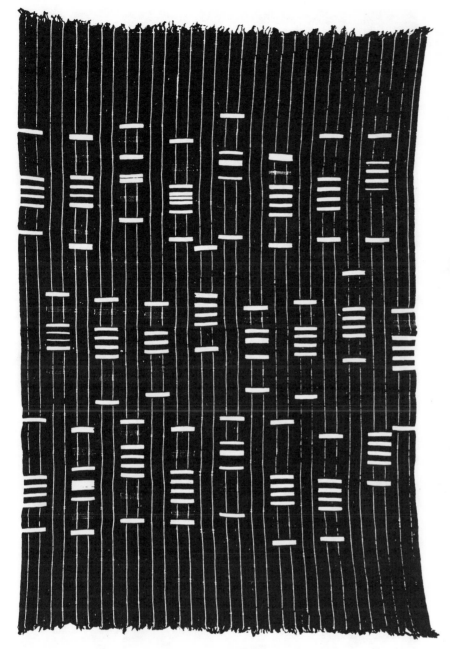

Right
Ewe cloth from
Ghana.

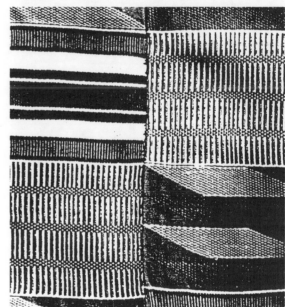

Right above, middle
Woven strips of cloth
sewn together.
Ashanti, Ghana.

Right
Weave from Upper
Volta.

Far right
Weave from the Ibo.

Above
Ashanti weaving
from Ghana.

Top right
Painted costume
from the Ivory Coast.

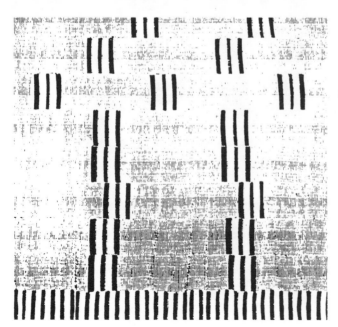

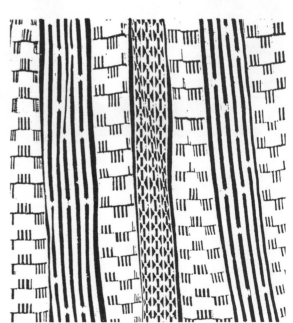

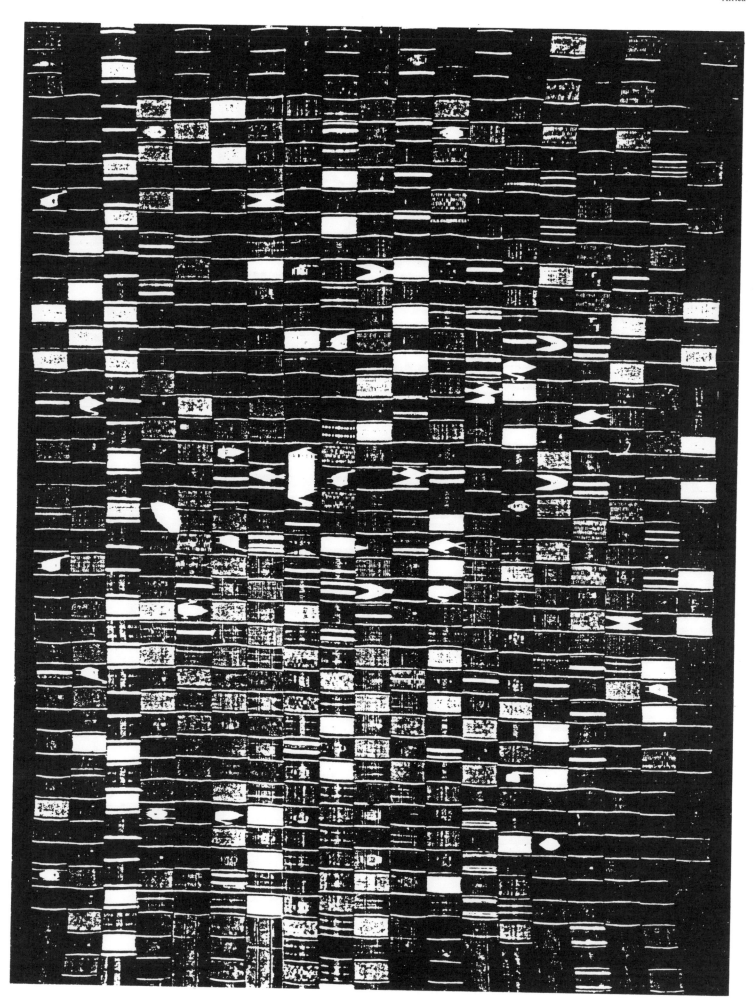

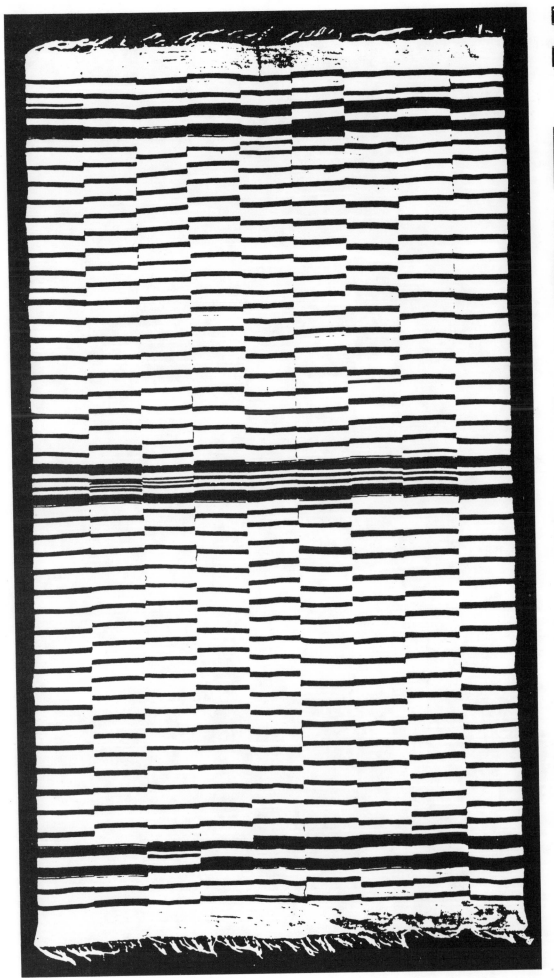

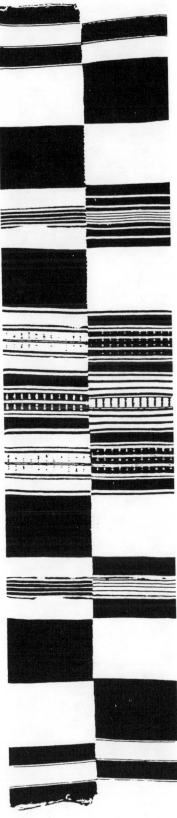

Left
Edge-sewn strip weave from Upper Volta.

Above
Strip weaving from Guinea.

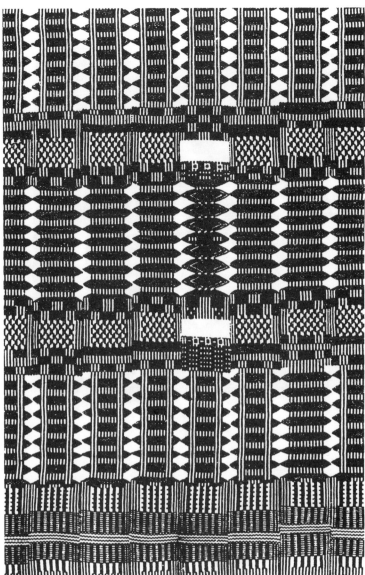

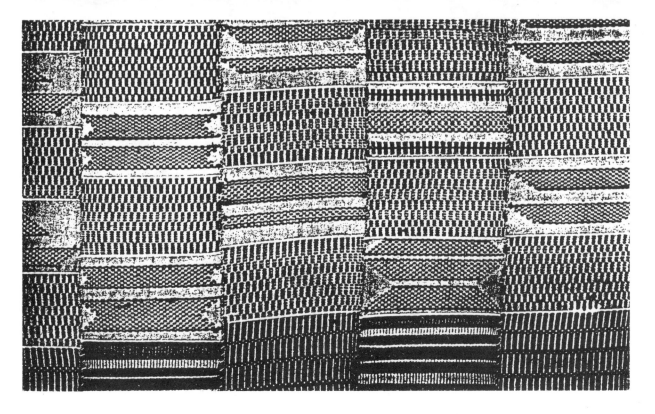

Above, left
Strip weave from
Mali.

Above
Woven cloth from
Nigeria.

Left
Woven cloth from
Ghana.

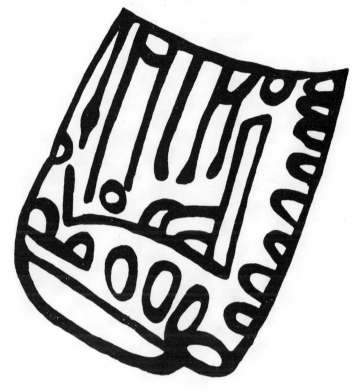

Above left
Ceremonial wooden
chair back, Ghana.

Above right
Bushman wall
painting, Rhodesia.

Middle left pair
Wooden stool
decorated with wire,
Kenya and bronze
bracelet, Mali.

Middle right pair
Ashanti brass lid,
Ghana and mud
relief pattern on wall
of house, Nigeria.

Below left
Tusi sewn matting
screen, Rwanda.

Below right
Bambara design on
cloth, Mali.

Above left
Wooden stool
decorated with wire,
Kenya.

Above right pair
Carved altar slab,
Dahomey and carved
grave stone, Nigeria.

Middle left
Carved design on
wooden spoon,
Congo-Kinshasa.

Middle right pair
Painted wooden
shield, Kenya, and a
decorated hide fan
from Nigeria.

Below left pair
Chiseled design on
wooden door latch,
Mali and painted
wall design, South
Africa.

Below right pair
Painted hide shield,
Kenya and wall
design, South Africa.

Above left pair
Painted wooden
mask, Cameroon and
wooden mask,
Congo-Kinshasa.

Above right pair
Ivory bracelet, Ivory
Coast and wooden
sculpture, Gabon.

Middle left pair
Wooden mask,
Nigeria and wood,
brass and copper
icon, Gabon.

Middle right pair
Wooden masks,
Ivory Coast, Mali,
Upper Volta.

Below left pair
Wooden mask,
Congo-Kinshasa and
dung covered
calabash mask,
Sudan.

Above
Painted wooden
mask, Congo.

Above left pair
Wooden water spirit
mask, Nigeria and
china-clay and wood
mask, Gabon.

Above middle pair
Painted wooden
mask, Congo-
Kinshasa and bronze
double-faced mask,
Ivory Coast, Mali,
Upper Volta.

Middle pair right
Wooden masks,
Congo.

Below right
Painted wooden
dance mask, Congo.

Below left
Wooden mask,
Nigeria.

Above left
Carved ivory design
of feeding elephant,
Nigeria.

Above right pair
Carved ivory catfish
design, Nigeria and
gold weight in fish
form, Ghana.

First row
Scraped calabash dog
design, Ghana, cattle
design, Dahomey
and engraved gourd
hunting scene,
Sudan.

Second row
Carved soapstone
zebra and monkey
designs, Zimbabwe
and pelicans with
turtle emblem found
on wooden door,
Ivory Coast, Mali,
Upper Volta.

Below left
Woven mat antelope
design, Congo.

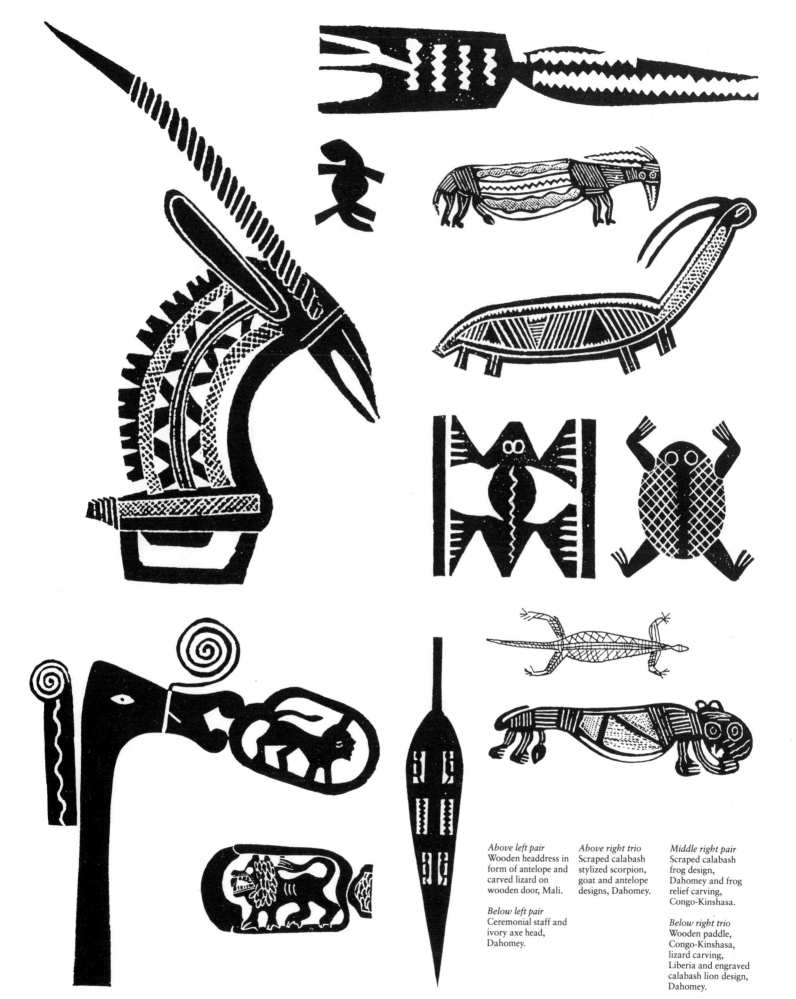

Above left pair
Wooden headdress in form of antelope and carved lizard on wooden door, Mali.

Below left pair
Ceremonial staff and ivory axe head, Dahomey.

Above right trio
Scraped calabash stylized scorpion, goat and antelope designs, Dahomey.

Middle right pair
Scraped calabash frog design, Dahomey and frog relief carving, Congo-Kinshasa.

Below right trio
Wooden paddle, Congo-Kinshasa, lizard carving, Liberia and engraved calabash lion design, Dahomey.

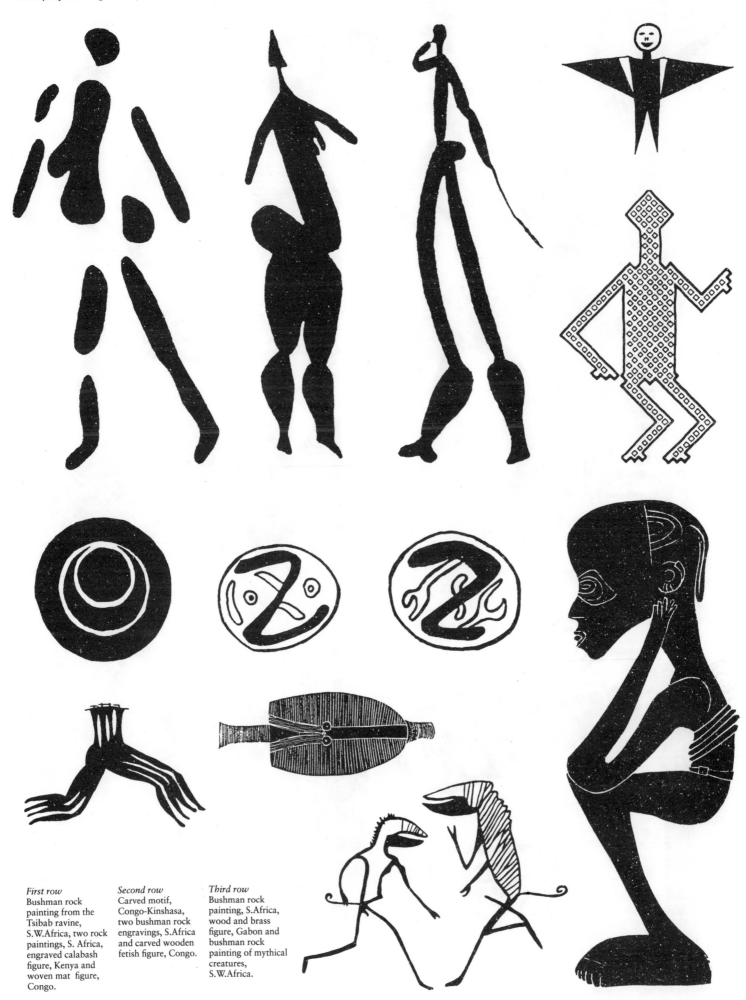

First row
Bushman rock
painting from the
Tsibab ravine,
S.W.Africa, two rock
paintings, S. Africa,
engraved calabash
figure, Kenya and
woven mat figure,
Congo.

Second row
Carved motif,
Congo-Kinshasa,
two bushman rock
engravings, S.Africa
and carved wooden
fetish figure, Congo.

Third row
Bushman rock
painting, S.Africa,
wood and brass
figure, Gabon and
bushman rock
painting of mythical
creatures,
S.W.Africa.

Below left pair
Wooden guardian
figures, Guinea and
Gabon.

Below right
Bushman rock
painting, S.W.Africa.

Above left
Three bushman rock
engravings, S.Africa.

Above right
Bushman rock
painting of fantastic
creature, Rhodesia.

73

Above left
Gold weight in bird form, Ghana.

Above right pair
Bushman rock painting of double-headed snake, S.Africa and brass relief bird design, Ghana.

Middle left
Scraped calabash bird designs, Dahomey.

Middle right pair
Scraped calabash snake and lizard design, Dahomey.

Below left
Carved lizard design on wooden door, Ivory Coast, Mali and Upper Volta.

Below right trio
Carved turtle design, Mali, scraped calabash bird design, Dahomey and gold weight in form of chameleon, Ghana.

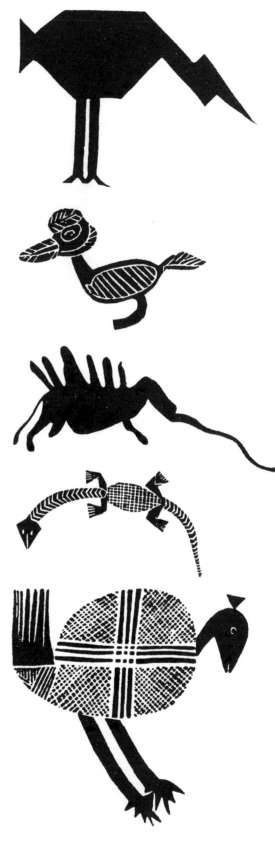

Right
Scraped calabash
snake and lizard
design, Ghana.

Middle left
Scraped calabash
cattle design,
Dahomey.

Below left
Scraped calabash
lizard design,
Dahomey.

Top
Woven mat bird
design, Congo and
carved bird design,
Mali.

Middle right pair
Rock painting of
mythical elephant,
Rhodesia and
scraped lizard design,
Dahomey.

Below right
Carved bird design
on wooden door,
Nigeria.

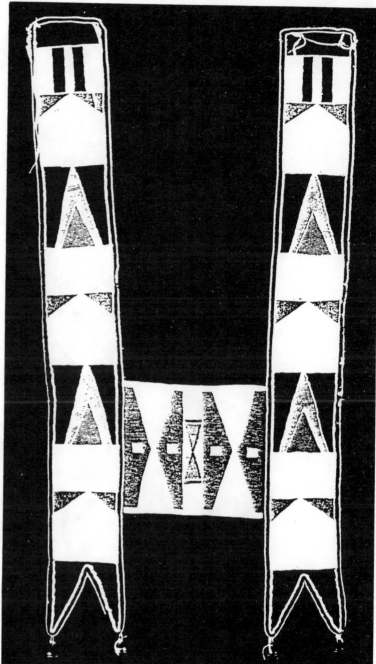

Far left
Three Acoma seed jars.

Left
Hopi blanket.

Above
Crow horse accoutrement.

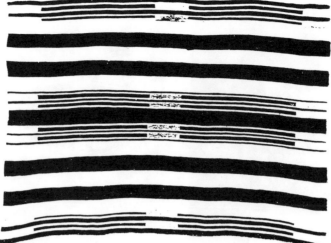

Far left
Pueblo jar.

Left
Navajo blanket.

Above left
Chilkat tunic.

Above right
Navajo saddle
blanket.

Bottom left
Detail of Chilkat
tunic.

Bottom right
Zuni bowl.

77

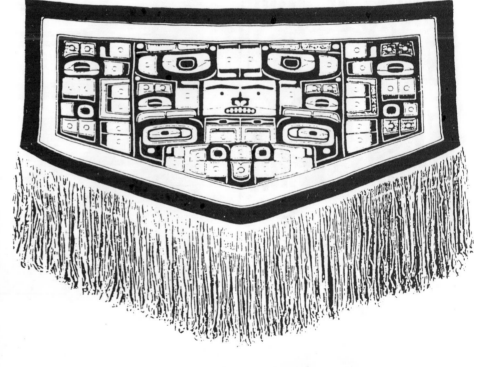

Above
Hopi Dance-wands.

Top and middle right
Chilkat blankets.
19th Century.

Right
Panamint basket.

Top row
Hopi, Eskimo and
Japanese
pictographs.

*Second row from left
to right*
Pictographic
drawings from the
Colorado, Ojibwa,
Cree, Mandan, Oto,
Pawnee and
Comanche.

*Third row from left
to right*
Horses drawn by
Mandan, Crow and
Cheyenne followed
by an Iroquois image
of war victims.

*Above, from left to
right*
Comanche horse and
rider, Sioux drawing
of horse with two
humans, and a
Kiowa wall drawing.

Right
A Navajo riding
blanket.

Top left
Pima basket.

Top right
Zia jar.

Far left
Paiute basket.

Near left
Washoe basket.

Left
Hopi ceremonial
textile design.

Above
Haida blanket
decorated with
affixed buttons.

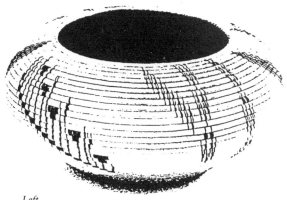

Left
Decorated Kwakiutl
dance apron.

Above
Washoe basket.

Below
Shell badge.

Left
Apache basket.

Above
Pueblo jar.

This page
Decorated pottery
from San Ildefonso.

Opposite page
Contemporary
painting drawing on
traditional Pueblo
imagery.

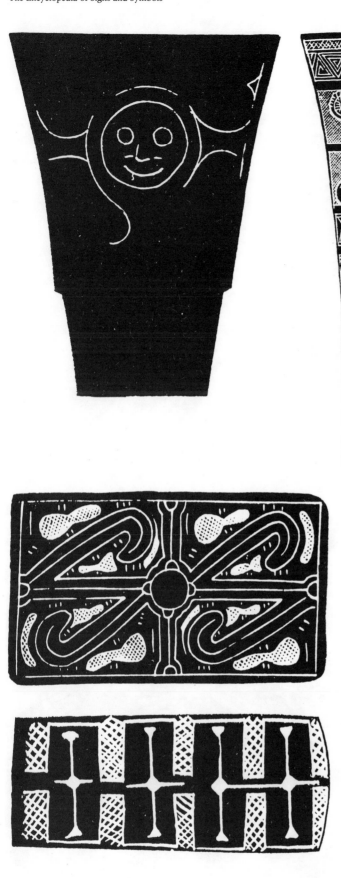

This spread
Equatorial South
American
wood-carving.

This spread
Carving from the
Amazon Basin.

This spread
Wood carving from
Amazon Indian
peoples.

89

This spread
Motifs carved in
wood from
Equatorial South
America.

Opposite page
Woven figure, Peru.

Above
Woven mask, Peru.

Left
Bird motif on
Peruvian bowl.

This page, above left
Woven llamas or
guanacos. These
animals were used
both for transport
and for their wool.

Above
Birds hunting for
food. Peru.

Left
Woven bird. Peru.

Opposite page
Woven lizards, Peru.

Embroidered, crested
birds, Peru.

Above
Woven cloth with
serpents and other
animals.

Right
Woven bird symbols
from Peru.

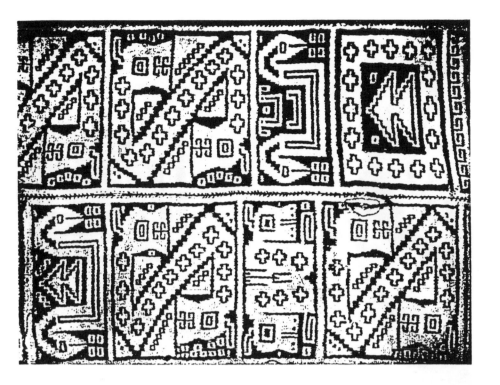

*Left top, middle and
bottom*
Textiles with stylized
animals and serpents.

*Above top, middle
and bottom*
Birds used as motifs
in Peruvian textiles.

Left and above
Symbols representing movement from Tabasco and Teotihuacan.

Above
Figure from Quintana Roo.

Left and below
Toltec figures.

Above
Movement sign from western Mexico.

Above
Toltec motif.

Left
Movement signs
from Huastec and
Tabasco.

This page
Various bird motifs
from Veracruz,
Guerrero, Cuautitlan
and western Mexico.

This page
Further bird motifs including an eagle, left. From Colima, Guerrero and Zempoala, Mexico.

Above
Monkey's head from
Veracruz.

Above right
Monkey from
western Mexico.

Above far right
Baby monkey, also
from western
Mexico.

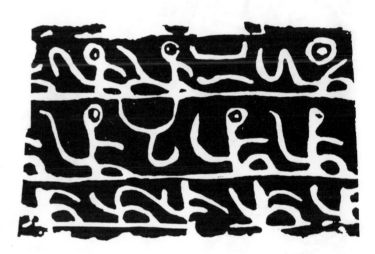

Far left
Monkey in the act of
mocking a bird.

Near left
Startled monkey
from western
Mexico.

Above
Formalized frieze
based on monkey
forms. Mexico.

Above
Various bird motifs.
Huastec. Mexico.

*Top, middle and
lower right*
Monkeys. Mexico.

Right
Monkey and man.
Mexico.

Above top
Dog from Veracruz.

Above middle
Huastec dog.

Above
Zempoala dog.

Left
Another dog from
Zempoala, Mexico.

Above
Mexican frog motifs
originating from
Zempoala, Huastec,
Veracruz, Michoacan
and Tlatilco.

Above top
Cuautitlan dog.

Above middle
Zempoala dog.

Above and left
Deer from
Zempoala, Mexico.

This page
Various animal
marks, including an
armadillo from
Remojadas
immediately to the
right.

This page
Motifs from
Cuautitlan, Veracruz
and Guerrero.

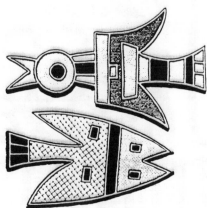

Above
Incised cat forms on a ceremonial ornament.
Rio Grande culture, Late Paracas period.

Left
Figures decorating an ancient Peruvian jar.

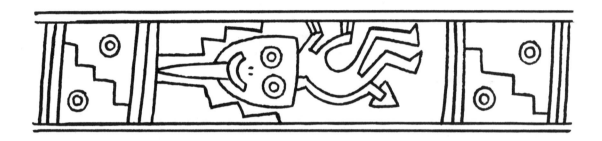

This page
Demons, killer
whales, fish and a
trophy head on a
Peruvian jar.

Above
The god of the
underworld,
Mictlantecuhtli.

Above left
Condor with snakes
in its talons.

Left
God flying with
captured human
heads.

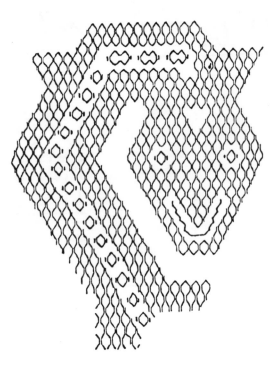

Left
A demon disguised
as a serpent.

Right
Woven snake. Peru.

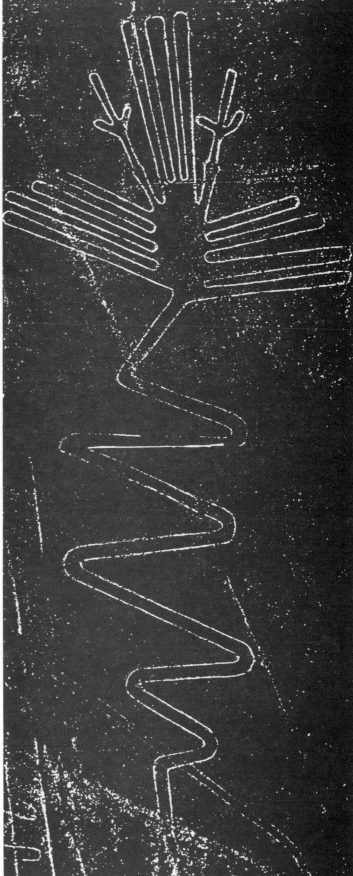

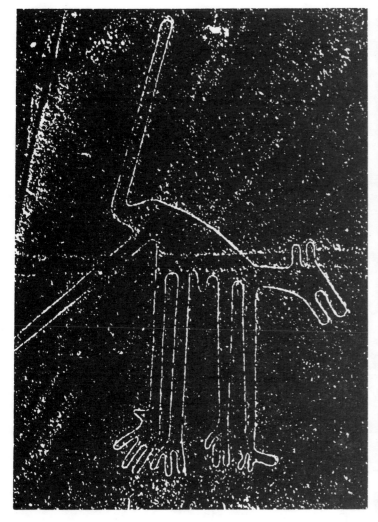

Above
A god with snakes in
his hair. A tomb
decoration.

Right
Bird with snake's
neck. Nazca.

Top
Nazca dog with long
legs.

111

Above
Small and large birds
as attendants to
human figures
emblazon a Nazca
poncho or cloak.

Left
Decorated Peruvian
textile used for
ceremonial garments.

Top left
Peruvian fish demon.

Left
Highly stylised bird.

Above
Coiled serpent from
Peru.

Above
Two monkeys
dancing. From the
Mexican State of
Tabasco.

Above
Painted panel from
Peru.

Top
Decoration on the
rear of a mirror
showing a man
hunting a bird.

Below
From a Mexican
spinning wheel.

Top
Image from a clay
stamp, possibly
representing a period
in the Aztec calendar.

Bottom
Dancing figure in the
form of an ape. From
a ceramic bowl.

Left
The goddess of
fertilty,
Xochiquetzal, who
was the mother of
Quetzalcoatl.

Above
An eagle decorating
a clay stamp from
the Axtec city of
Tenochtitlan.

Right
Image of a leaping
animal. From a
ceramic bowl.

Above
The god of fire,
Huehueteotl.

Right
Mayan hieroglyphics
representing dates or
times of the year.

Above
Various mythical
animal motifs from
Mexico before the
conquest by Spain.

Above
Varying degrees of
abstraction from the
form of a dog.

Above
Two more examples
of the decorative dog
motif. Mexico.

Above
Turkey-like bird,
probably a buzzard,
used to decorate
Mexican pottery
prior to European
colonization.

117

Below
Mochica ceramic
motifs of crustacean
with a human head
and startled bird.

Above top
Stylised bird on a
Nazca pot.

Above
Stylised reptile from
Mochica pot.

Right top
Early Nazca pot with
otter head .

Right middle
Cat decoration on
Nazca pot.

Right bottom
Killer whale with
human arm. Nazca.

Top
Puma. Peru.

Right
Rio Grande killer
whale decoration.

Far right
Rio Grande fish.

Right
Sculpted bird of prey
from Chavin de
Huantar.

Below
Bas-relief figure of a
god bearing the fangs
of a hunting cat.
Chavin culture.

Below right
Cat depicted on a
frieze at Chavin de
Huantar.

119

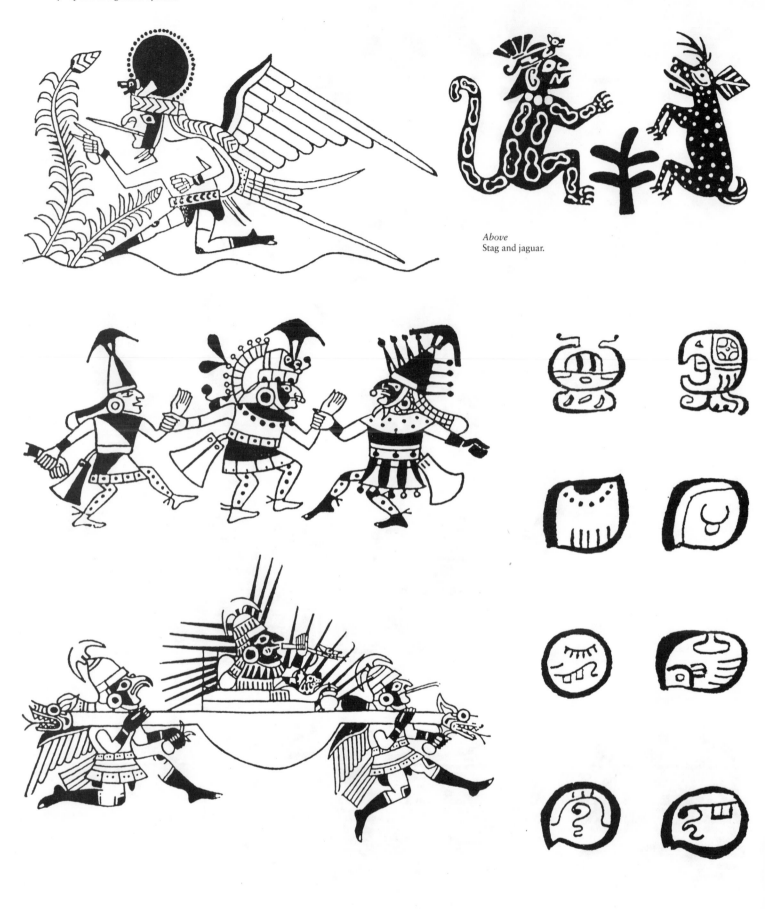

Above
Stag and jaguar.

Top
Mythical figure
running.

Middle
Warriors dancing
with bells and
ornamental
head-dresses.

Bottom
A god being borne in
a sedan-chair.

Right
Mayan hieroglyphics
representing dates
and times of the year.

120

Above
Capturing an enemy.
Nakedness as a
symbol of defeat.

Above
Dancing god in the
form of ape and
crocodile from
Panama.

Left
Reptilian form from
a ceramic bowl.
Panama.

Right
Mochica warriors
bearing the attributes
of a fox which,
because of its
associations with
fleetness and with
cunning, boded well
for a fighting man.

Left
A warrior bearing
the characteristics of
a hawk with the face,
tail, wings and talons
clearly identifiable.

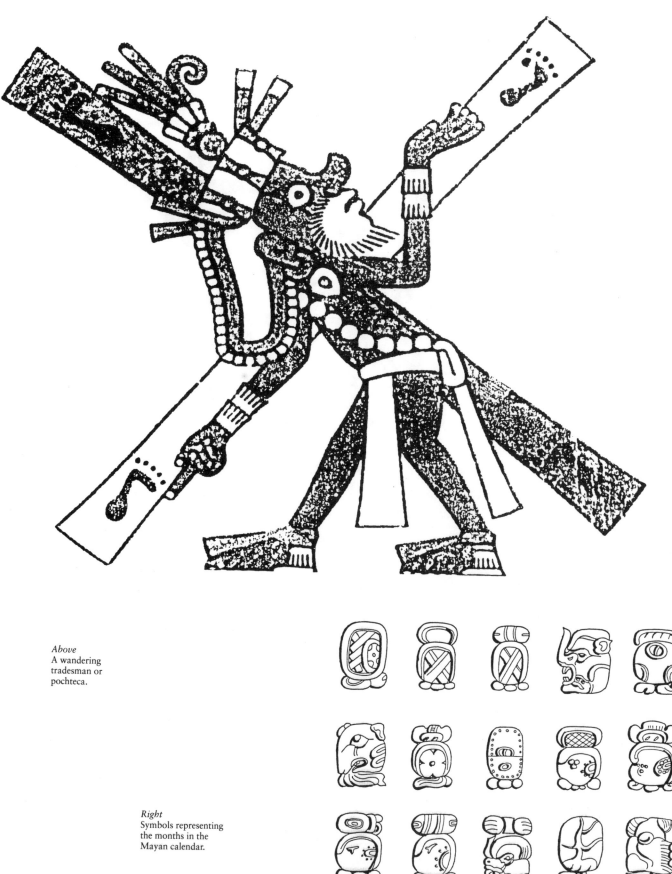

Above
A wandering
tradesman or
pochteca.

Right
Symbols representing
the months in the
Mayan calendar.

Left
An embroidered border with a main feature of a monkey with a serpent's tail. Inside its body is contained the figure of a cat. Other small animal figures fill in the background. Peruvian 'Necropolis' style.

Above and opposite page
Details from a Mayan manuscript.

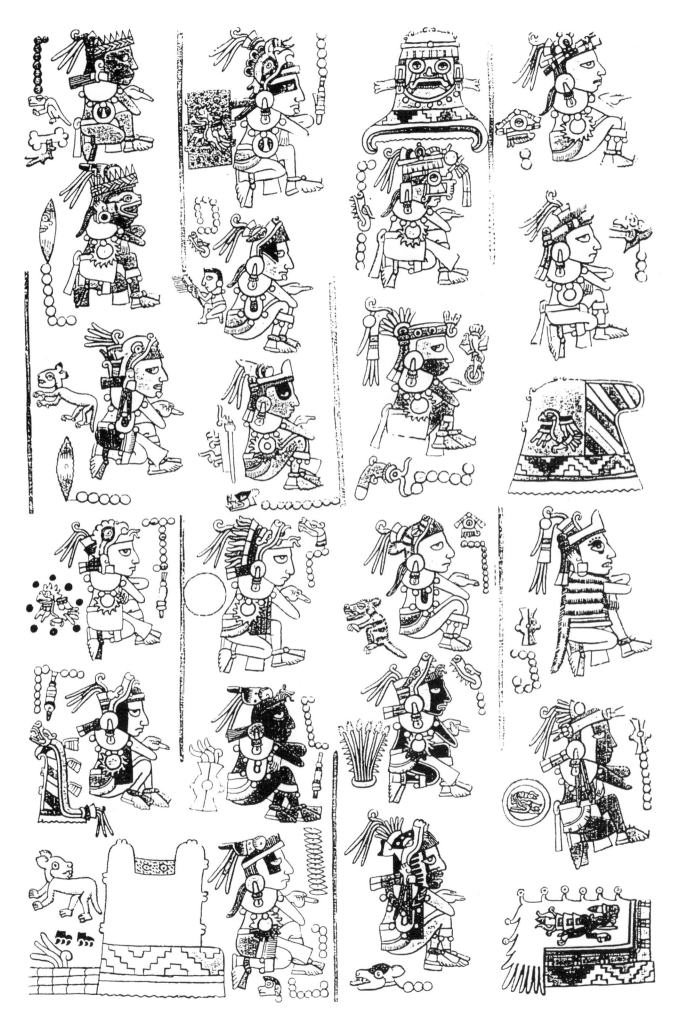

This spread
Figures from an
ancient Mayan
manuscript.

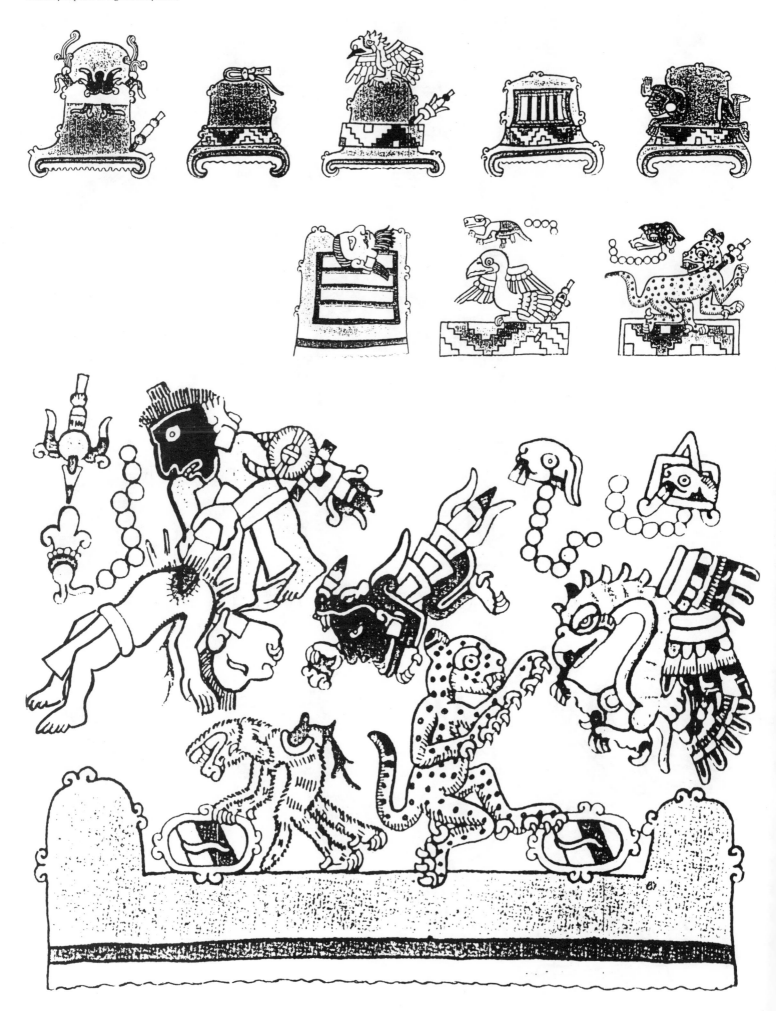

This spread
Details from Mayan
manuscript.

This spread
Details from a
Mayan manuscript.

Middle left top and bottom
Bronze working from the Shang Dynasty. c. 1500BC.

Near left
Silver and gold inlay patterns from the Chou Dynasty in China. c. 800BC.

Above
Charcoal drawing from a hut in New Zealand.

Above
Bronze harness work from the Shang Dynasty. c. 1500BC.

Above
Lizard carved on an agricultural implement. New Zealand.

Above
Painted roof timber. New Zealand.

Left
From a jewel box.
New Zealand.

Above
New Zealand wood
carving of a female
ancestor suckling her
infant.

Above
A mythical creature
used as a common
motif in
New Zealand.

Above middle
From a gourd bowl.
New Zealand.

133

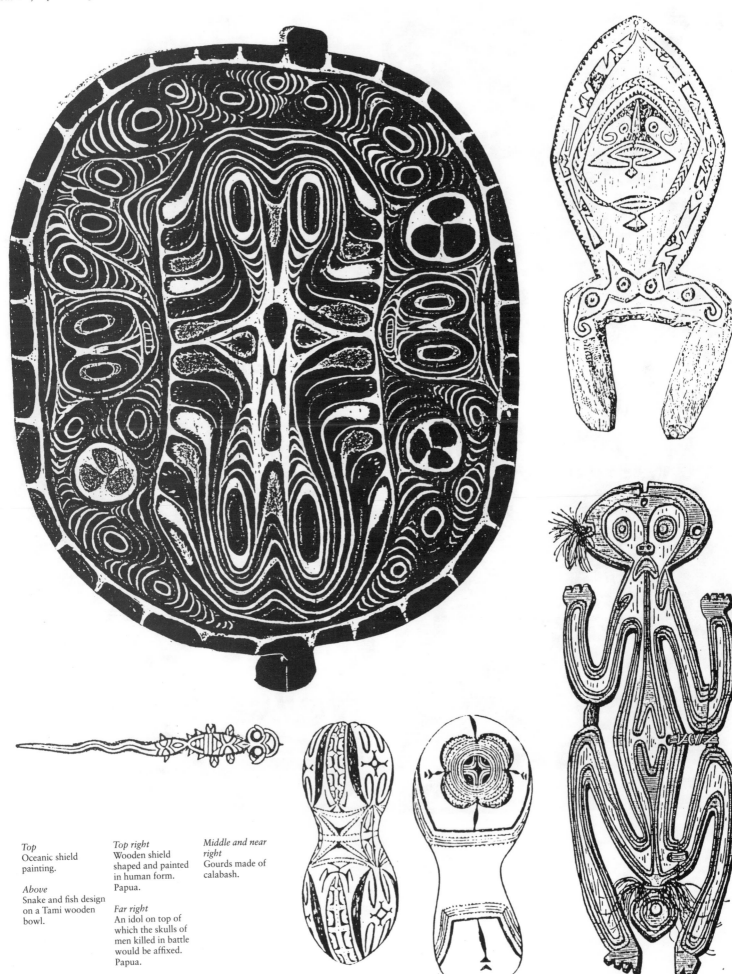

Top
Oceanic shield
painting.

Above
Snake and fish design
on a Tami wooden
bowl.

Top right
Wooden shield
shaped and painted
in human form.
Papua.

Far right
An idol on top of
which the skulls of
men killed in battle
would be affixed.
Papua.

*Middle and near
right*
Gourds made of
calabash.

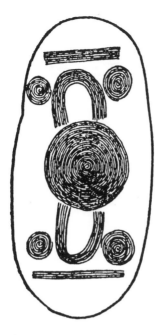

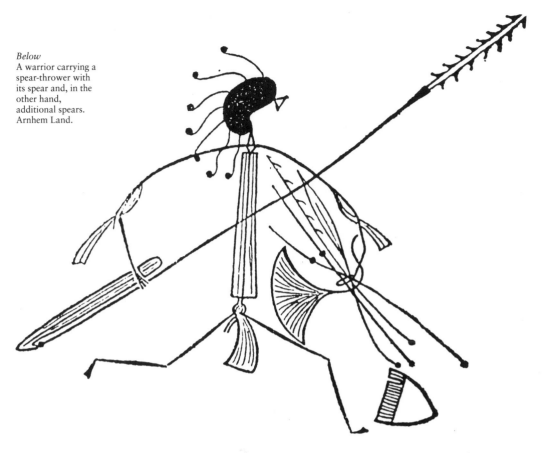

Below
A warrior carrying a spear-thrower with its spear and, in the other hand, additional spears. Arnhem Land.

Above
A women's totem object. Australia.

Left
Religious painting from a Sepik cult house.

Above
Sea-urchin motif. Hawaii

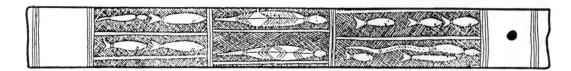

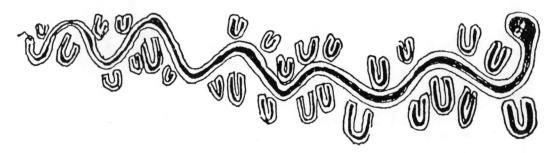

Left
Carved smoking
pipe. Australia.

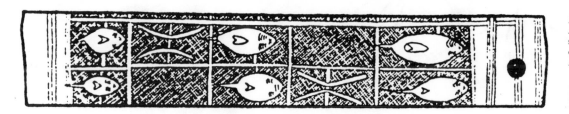

Left middle
A mythical snake
surrounded by bands
of wild dogs. Central
Australia.

Left
Smoking pipe.
Northern Australia.

Above
Decoration from a
mask made of bark
worn by Papuan
men.

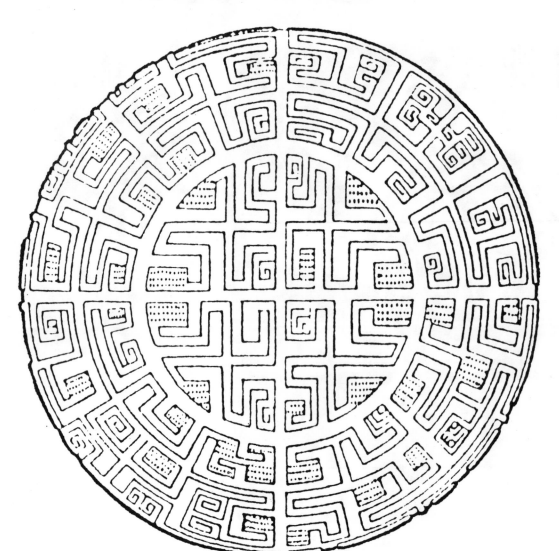

Left
Relief carving in a
wooden bowl from
the Marquesas
Islands.

136

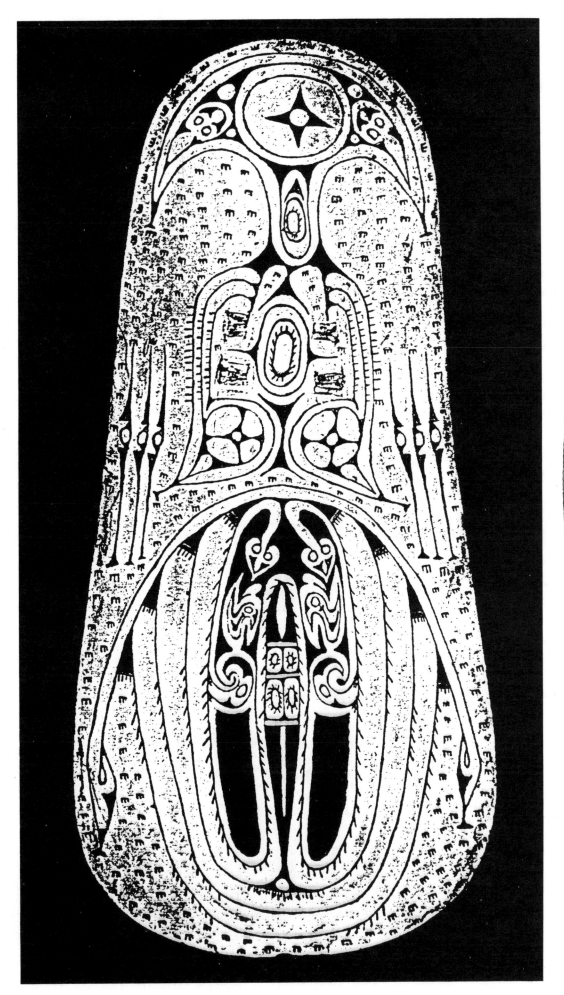

Above left
Spear-thrower from
South Australia.

Left
Painting on a
wooden shield from
the Trobriand
Islands.

Above
Sacred objects carved
with motifs of special
significance. North
Australia.

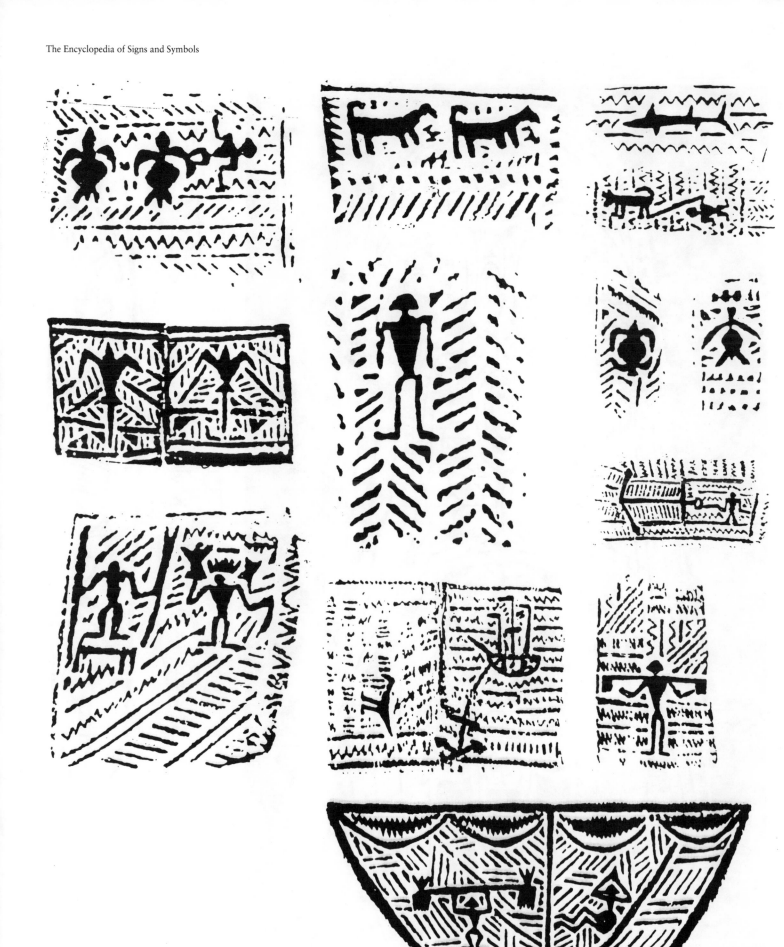

This page
Rubbings from
carved Tongan clubs.

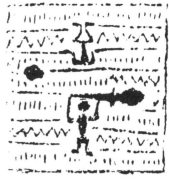

Left
Tongan club with
scenic engravings.
17th Century.

Above
Rubbings from
carved Tongan clubs.

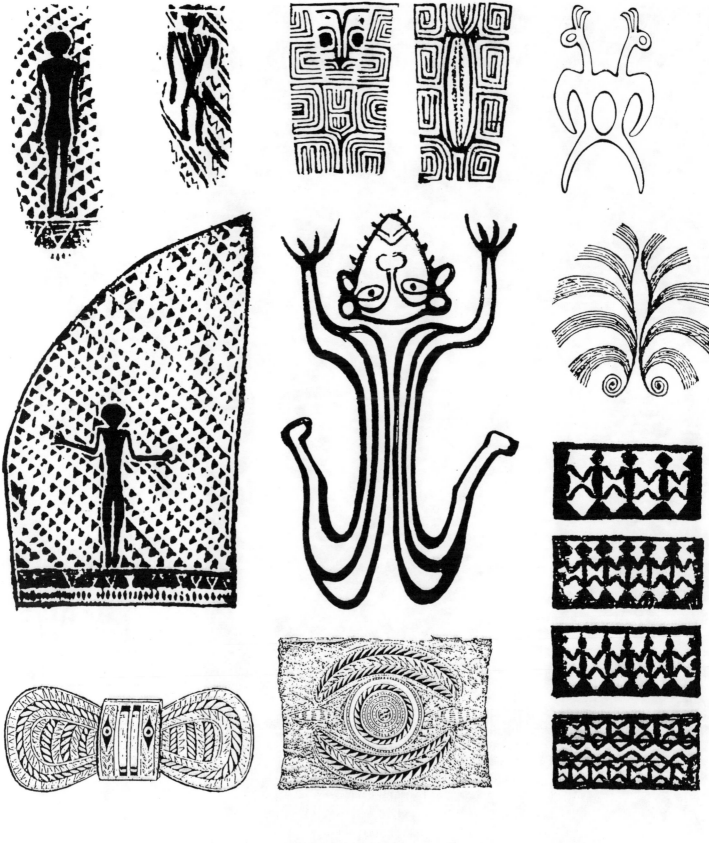

Top left, top right and middle
Silhouettes engraved on a Fijian war club.

Above
Wooden mask wing-shaped ears. New Ireland.

Top left and right
Engraved markings on a Marquesas bowl.

Above
Painted bark cloth. New Ireland.

Top and middle
Head motifs from Easter Island.

Above
Four motifs from a drum.

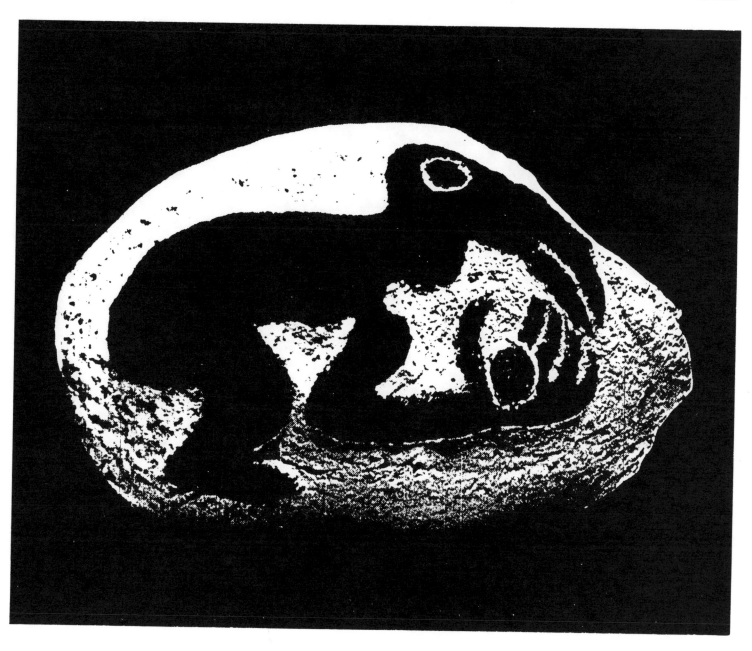

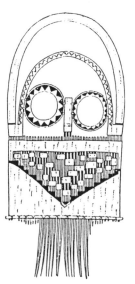

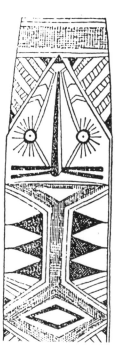

Top
Carved stone
showing a half bird,
half man being
holding an egg.
Easter Island.

Above
Ancestral panel.

Far right
Decorated club from
Santa Cruz Island.

Next right
Decorated comb
from Mussau Island.

Middle right
Painted wood panels
from Banks Island.
The faces and the
birds represent the
spirits of ancestors.

Immediate right
Carved and painted
paddle from the
Solomon Islands.

Top
A detail from a landscape made from gold inlaid into bronze. Han Dynasty.

Middle
Rosettes and a Han-silk animal.

Right
Mysterious carving of a snake copulating with a tortoise from a Han Dynasty tomb.

Far right
Part of a Han Dynasty star map showing what we call the Plough or Ursa Major.

Above
A jade disc.

Above
A phoenix on a
lacquer bowl.

Left
Two dragons.

Below
Silk work.

Above
A Han Dynasty
picture of paradise.

Right
A bird/dragon.

Top
Three pendants; the first is the bringer of wealth, the next employs the character of good fortune and the third wishes prosperity.

Left
The tiger was used by military officers as a symbol of fierceness and courage.

Above
In China the dragon has the positive attributes of spirituality and is a link with heaven. Hence the Chinese Emperors took this creature as their personal emblem.

Top left
Candlesticks bearing images of well-wishing.

Top right
An injunction on behalf of increased prosperity.

Above
The monkey King and the pig God.

Right
The pheasant symbolises beauty and good luck.

Papercuts.

Left
This papercut
employs two magpies
to offer double
happiness.

Above
Goldfish.

Right
Two carp.

Right
Papercuts utilising,
from top down, bird
and loquates, hen
and chicks, flowers
and birds and
swallows.

Left
Happy flowers.

Right
Papercut landscape with a pagoda and boats.

Middle row
The flowers bloom, abundant harvest and carp.

Above
Flowers of happiness.

Top left and right
Chrysanthemum, the
symbol of endurance.

Left above
Bonsai trees.

Left
Magpies, the birds of
happiness, unite with
the flower of spring.

Above
The phoenix is the
emblem of femininity
and the peony
represents wealth
and position.

Top left
Two
chrysanthemums.

Top right
The stag and the pine
tree both represent
longevity.

Far left
Two
chrysanthemums.

Left
Birds and floral
forms symbolising
happiness.

Above
A message wishing
long life upon the
recipient.

The lion not only represents strength and courage but it is also imbued with a playful and mischievous nature.

Left
The cock stands for courage and reliability.

Below left
A monkey smoking.

Below
Bringing home the harvest.

Middle row
Another cockerel, a lion as Buddhist Guardian, and a fisherman.

Far left
The Lion Dance.

Left
Two pigs bringing prosperity.

Above
Monkey carrying lanterns.

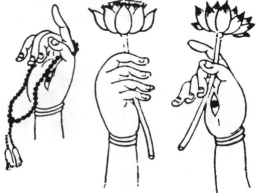

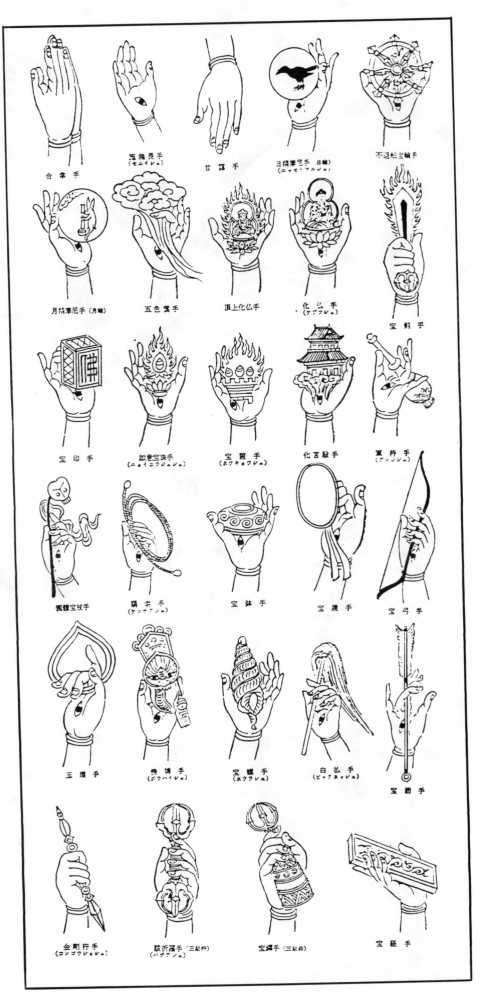

Top
Fudo.

Above and right
Drawings from the book of a thousand hands.

Opposite page
The letter 'A' which shapes and makes the Primal Sound.

धर्म चरकी

चोरका

विज्ञासि

नीली पीत

गर्दे बा सी

वाभराक्ष.

सूचनी

Left
From Rajasthan,
18th century.

*Below, left to right
and top to bottom*
Performing Fudo.
Stage one is to
assume the identity
of Fudo; next the
fists of anger turn to
the triangle of fire by
extending the
forefingers; drawing
the sword to destroy
demons - the right
hand is the sword
and the left is the
scabbard; the priest
has drawn the sword
and places the
scabbard on his head
- this signifies the
initial threat; he
replaces the sword
into its scabbard; he
draws the sword
again and, by
brandishing it,
purifies the Temple
and drives out the
demons; lastly,
having routed the
demons, he replaces
the sword once more
in its scabbard.

*Bottom, extreme
right*
One of the mudras of
Amida.

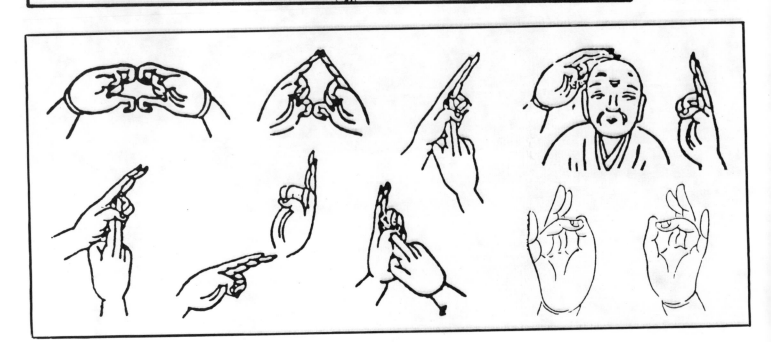

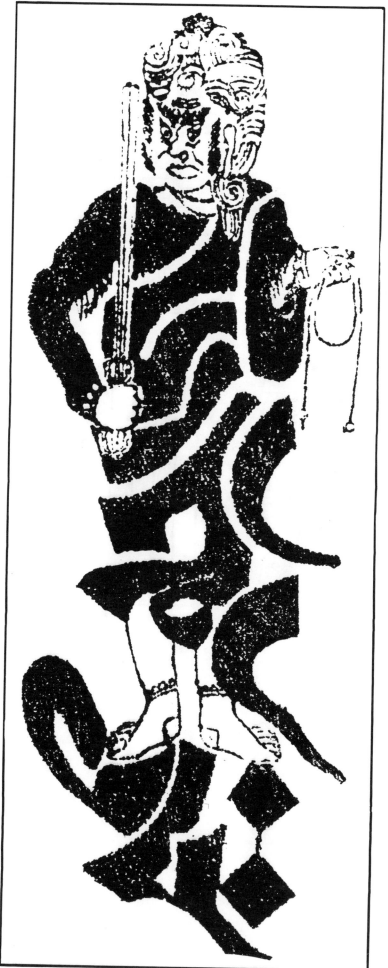

Above
The mudra for crushing evils.

Near right
Performing a mudra.

Far right
The body of Fudo is here formed from various Sanskrit letters.

Below
From Rajasthan. 18th century.

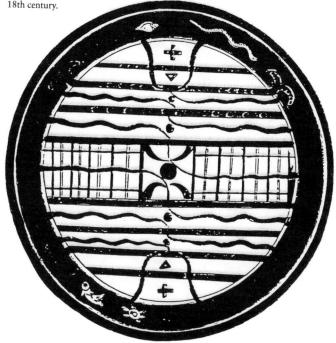

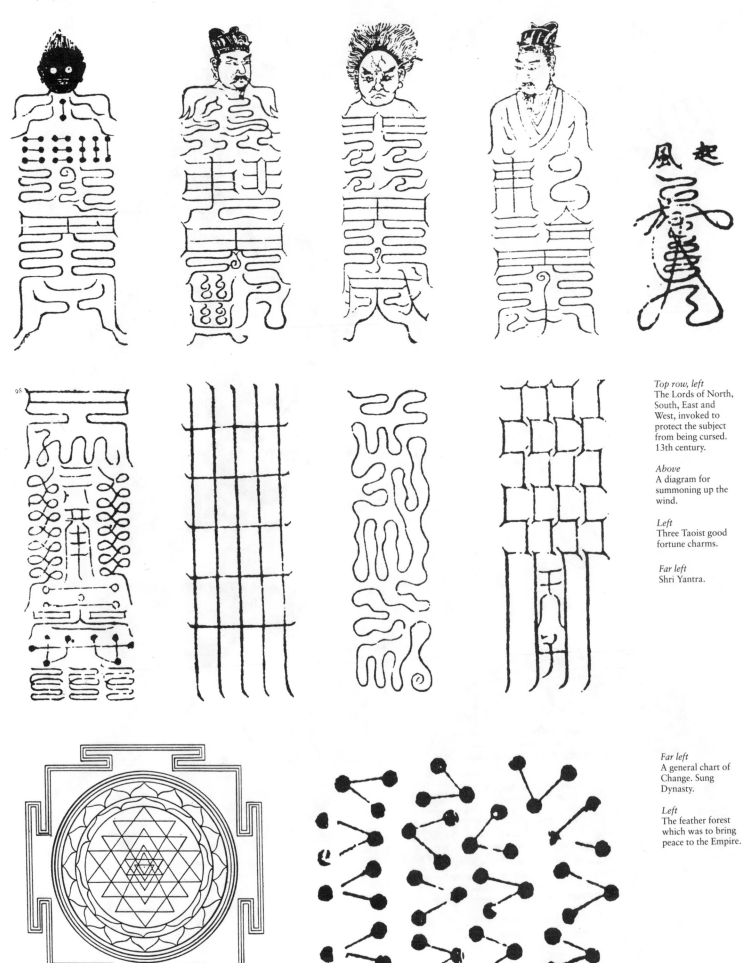

Top row, left
The Lords of North, South, East and West, invoked to protect the subject from being cursed. 13th century.

Above
A diagram for summoning up the wind.

Left
Three Taoist good fortune charms.

Far left
Shri Yantra.

Far left
A general chart of Change. Sung Dynasty.

Left
The feather forest which was to bring peace to the Empire.

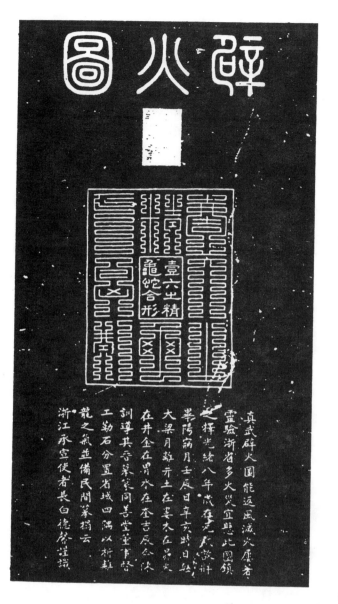

Far left
Chart for warding off fire.

Left
A charm for increasing mental energy.
Sung Dynasty.

Far left
Om.

Near left
The site of phallocentric energy.

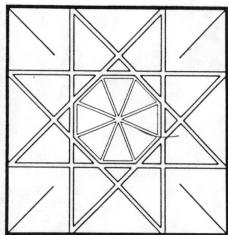

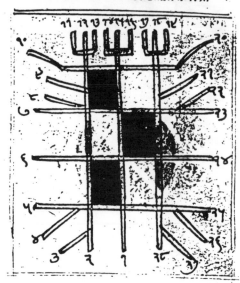

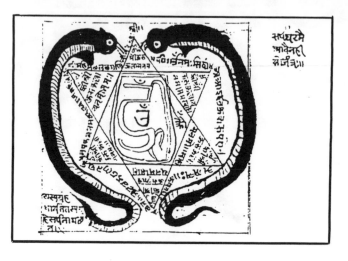

This page
Geometric devices
and mystic diagrams
for assisting the
effectiveness of
contemplation.

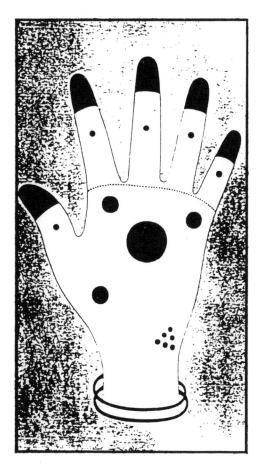

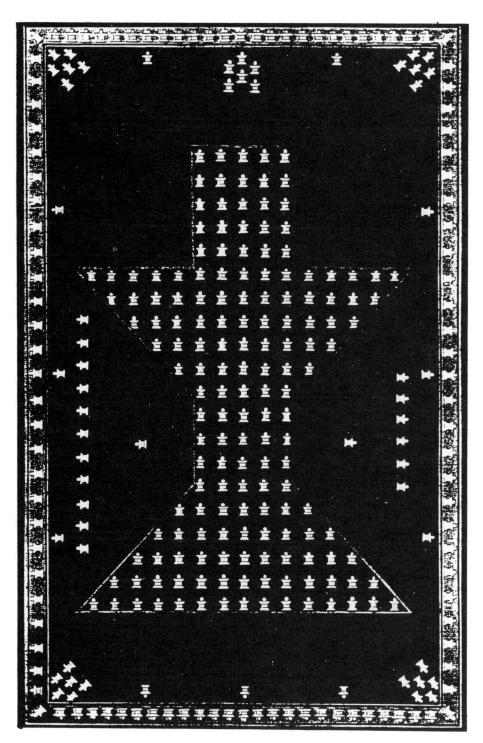

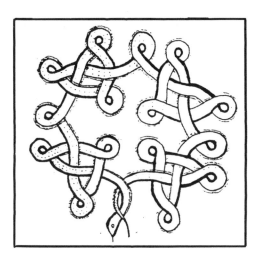

Top left
A diagram revealing the endless progression of change.

Middle left
Energy centres.

Left
Mystic contemplation diagrams and the eye in the hand.

Above
18th Century Rajasthan weaving.

159

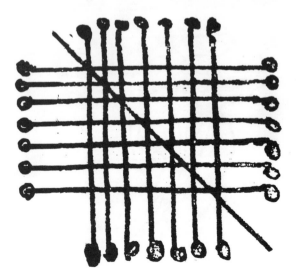

Above
Four Tibetan mandala yantras used to intensify the state of consciousness. 19th century.

Left
The monster of time.

Right
Esoteric Sung
Dynasty script.

Middle right
Songs from the
Taoist Canon.

Far right
A good-luck charm
frequently woven
into lattice patterns.

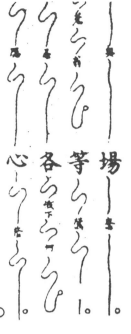

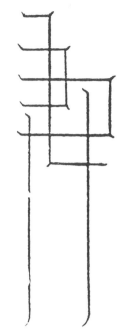

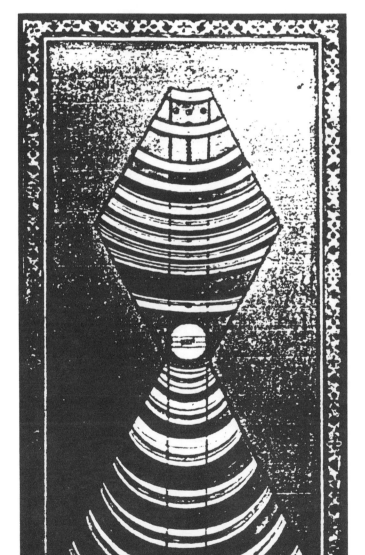

Far left
Matter radiating
through space.
19th century.

Above and left
Shri yantras.

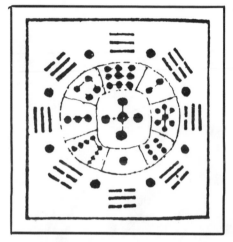

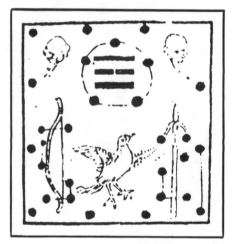

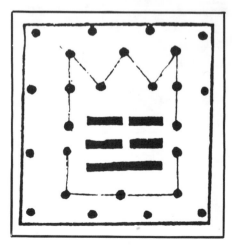

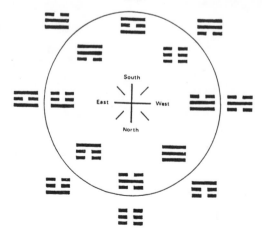

Far left
Four diagrams outlining the nature of the universe.

Left
Outside the circle is the Primal Heaven; inside the circle is the configuration of the Inner World.

Top
Eight trigrams circle around what was the yin/yang centre of a Ch'ing Dynasty bowl.

Above left
A Taoist vision of the Star God.

Top
The eight trigrams.

Near right
An inscribing for the removal of evil spirits. Sung Dynasty.

Middle right
A diagram revealing the workings of the yin aspect. Sung Dynasty.

Below
The penetration of the Essential Spirit, linking the smallest and the largest in Creation. Sung Dynasty.

Far right, top
The location of the vital centres of erotic energy. 18th century.

Far right, below
A calligraphicly embellished image of the Immortal God Liu-Hai. 19th century.

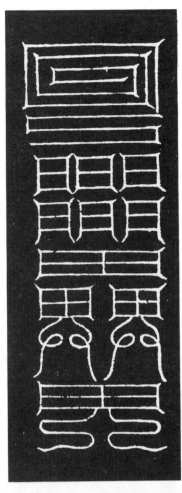

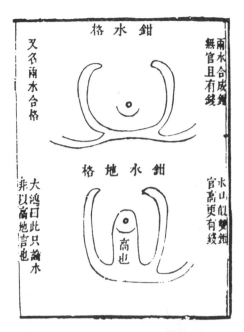

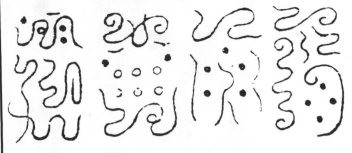

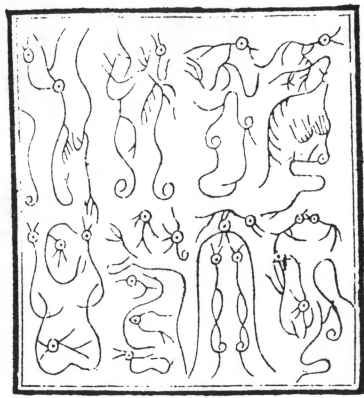

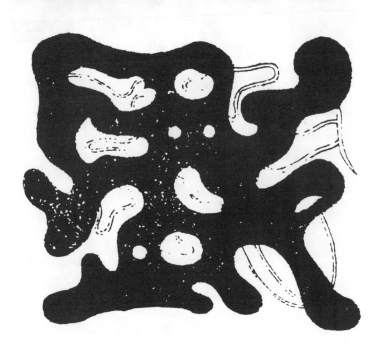

Above
Mystic scripts.

Far left
A map of the
Mountain of the
Heavenly Kingdom.

Right
Cranes,
representative of
long life, festoon this
16th century jar.

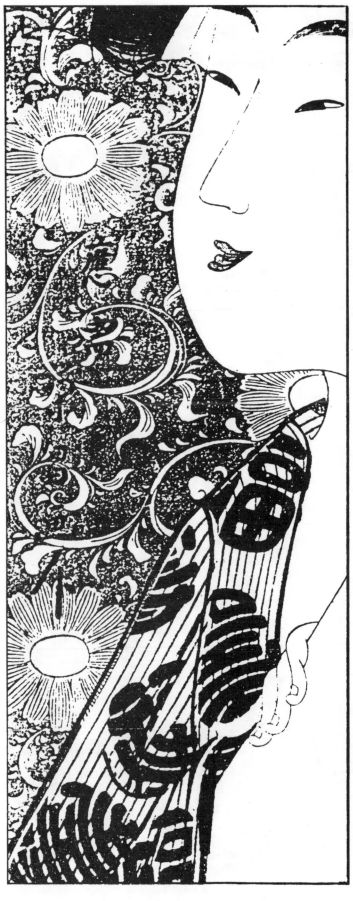

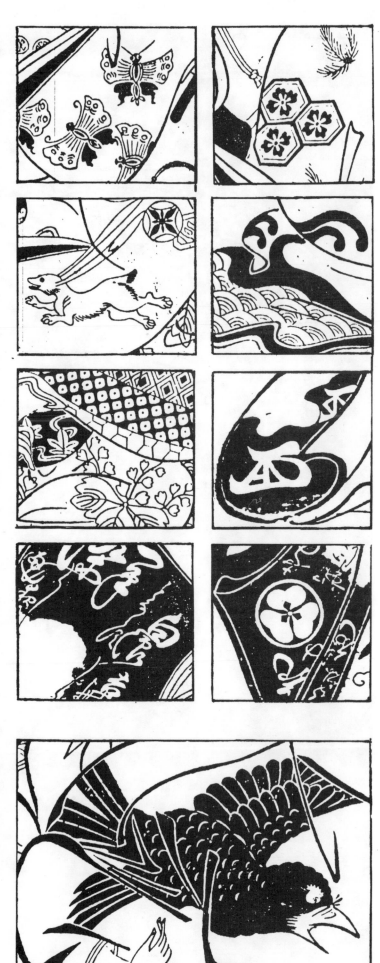

This spread
Decorative motifs
from Japanese prints.

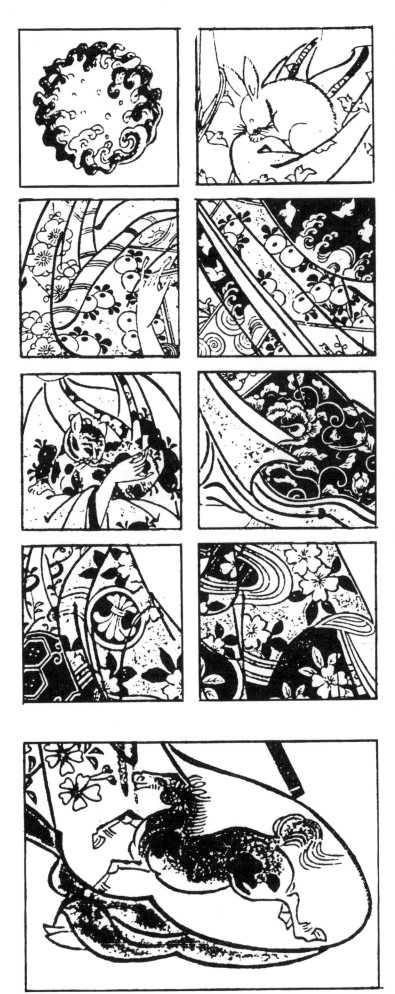

Left
Embroidered Noh
costume.

Below
Bamboo motif used
as a family crest.

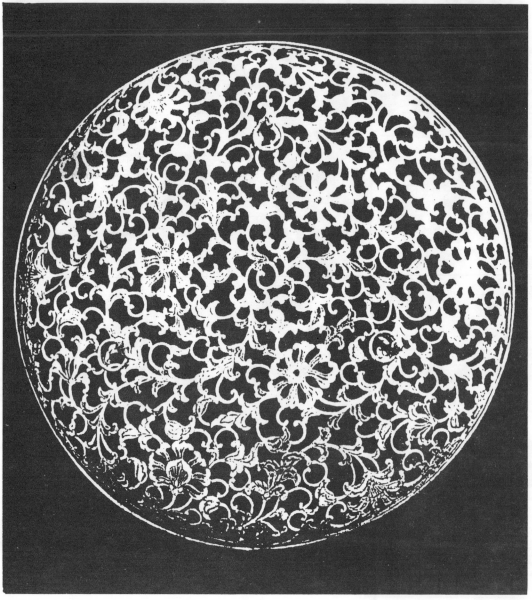

Left
Metal filigree work.

Above
Costume motifs from
the Edo period.

Above
Family crests from
the Edo and Meiji
periods. Motifs used
as follows:

Top row
Paving stone,
lightning and incense
symbol;

Second row
Interlocking rings,
circling 'comma' and
star motifs;

Third row
Diamond and chess
piece motifs;

Fourth row
Tortoise-shell and
chess-piece motifs;

Fifth row
Flower and diamond
motifs and the plum-
blossom emblem;

Sixth row
Gingko leaf and
crane.

Left
Inlaid lacquer work.

Above, top row
Family crests
and goose motifs;
Above
Family crests
utilising
calligraphic devices.
All from the Edo and
Meiji periods.

Left
Phoenix motif used
in brocade work.

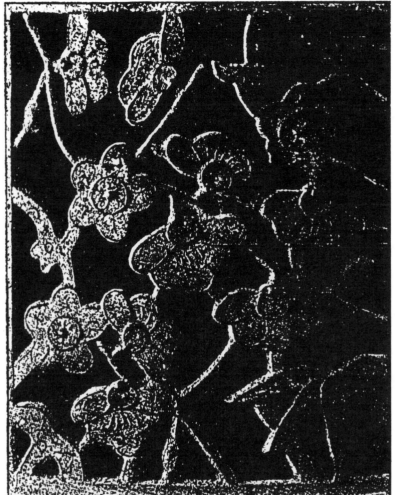

Top
Panel of a bronze
lantern using a
bamboo motif.

Above
Butterfly and melon
motif on paper.

Top
Plum-blossom motif
on a bronze lantern.

Middle and left
Brocade decoration.

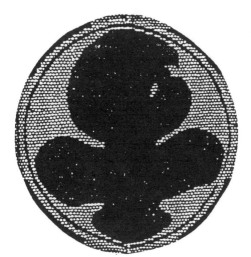

Left
Castle design from a
19th century bedding
cover.

Below
Wood-cut
symbolising birds in
the spring.

Above
Cherry blossom
motif.

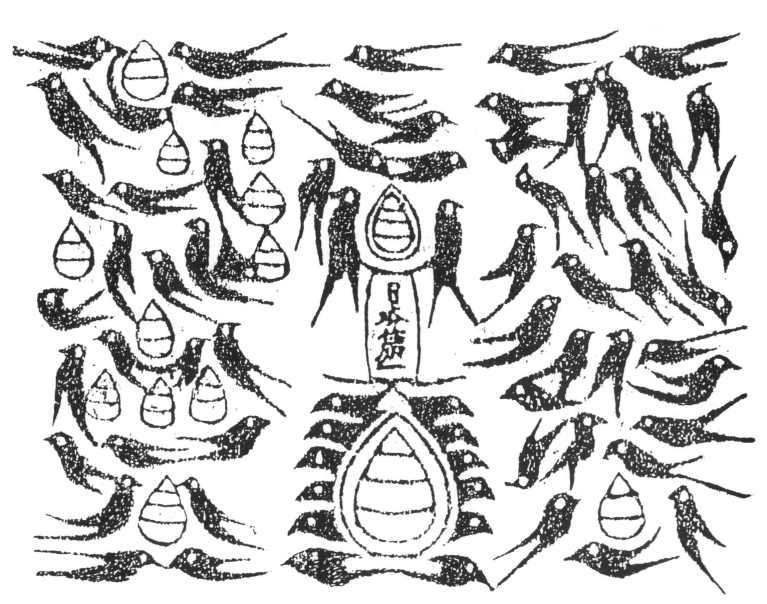

Below
Part of a bronze
ceremonial canopy.

Far left and left
Animal motifs on a
lacquer box.

*Top and middle pair
left*
Sword guards with
crane symbol, new
moon/wet grass,
cherry blossom
pattern and crab
emblems.

Middle pair to right
Details from wood
print.

Above
Detail from a lacquer
box.

174

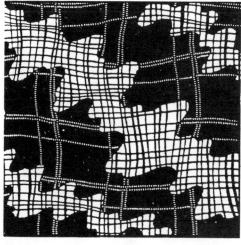

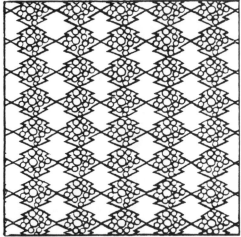

Above
Detail from lacquer
work.

*Right top, middle
and above*
Papercut patterns.

Right
Brocade work
employing the image
of a mythical bird.

Left
Lacquer box with bird and plant motifs.

Right
Brocade work with bird and leaf forms.

Right
Lacquer box with inlaid bamboo and grass decoration.

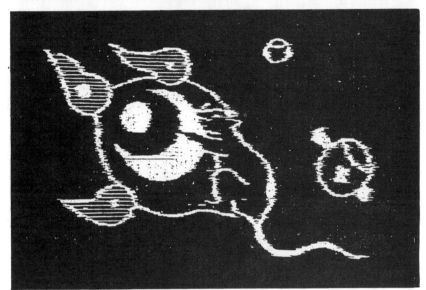

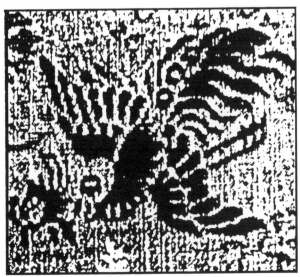

Above left
Textile, peony and
Chinese lion motifs.

Above right
Textile, featuring
Kotobuki symbol
(for long-life and
fortune) and long-
tailed tortoise.

Middle left
Textile, floral
pattern.

Middle right
Textile, mouse and
gems.

Below left
Decorative brocade
work.

Below right
Part of textile,
symmetrical birds
motif.

177

Above and below left
Paper-cut patterns.

Above
A round "shou"
encircled by bats.

Middle
Metal wash-basin
with "shou" motif.

Below
Butterfly motif on
sides of basin.
Bat motif on rim of
basin.

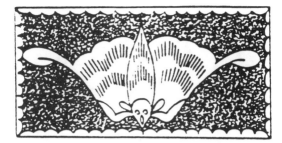

Above
Flying bat from a brass tray.

Middle
Versions of the character "fu" meaning "happiness".

Below
Butterfly decoration, emblem of marital bliss and joy and bat motif portraying happiness.

Above and below right
Paper-cut patterns.

179

Right and below
Papercuts.

Far right, top down
Variations of the
"shou" character
utilising the
swastika: from a
textile design; from a
brass furniture
fitting; from a design
on a wooden box;
with attendant
ribbons.

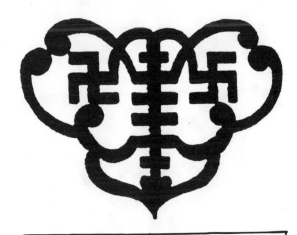

Left and below
Papercuts.

Far left, top down
From a carpet design; the mythical chimera from an embroidered silk; from textile designs; a dragon from a brass vessel; a border from a candlestick.

181

Above and below left
Paper-cut patterns.

Above right
Variations on the "shou" character which signifies 'longevity'.

Middle right
More versions found on textiles, china and the like except central design (enlarged) which would be used as a door handle.

Below right
Written character of "shou".

Above and below left
Paper-cut patterns.

Above and middle right
Variations on the "shou" character and borders.

Below right
Medallion incorporating "shou" and blossom border.

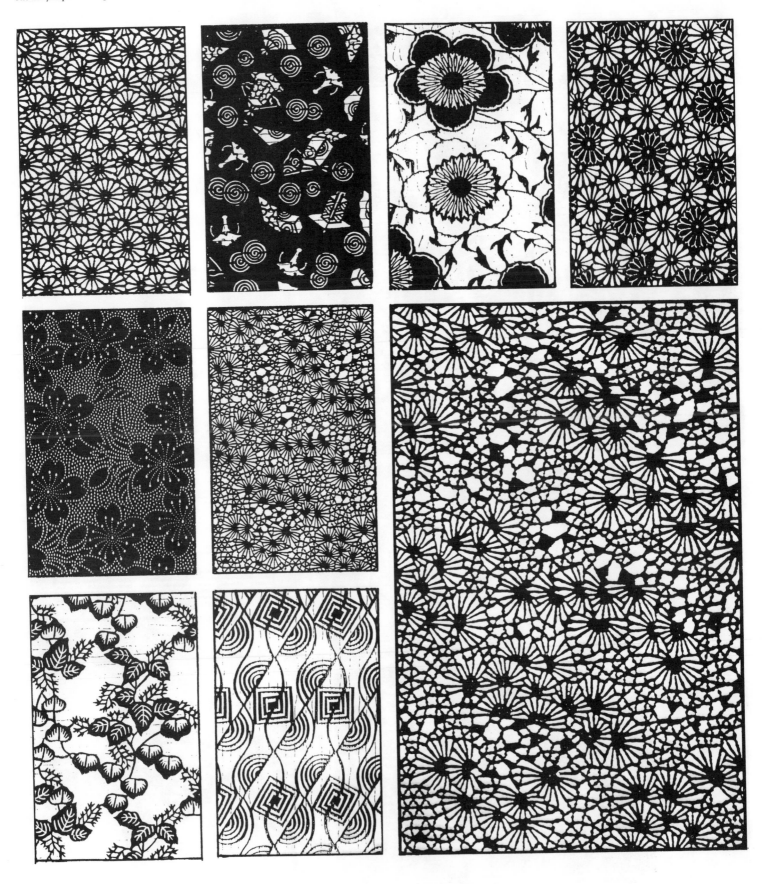

This spread
Japanese paper with
stencil cut designs.

185

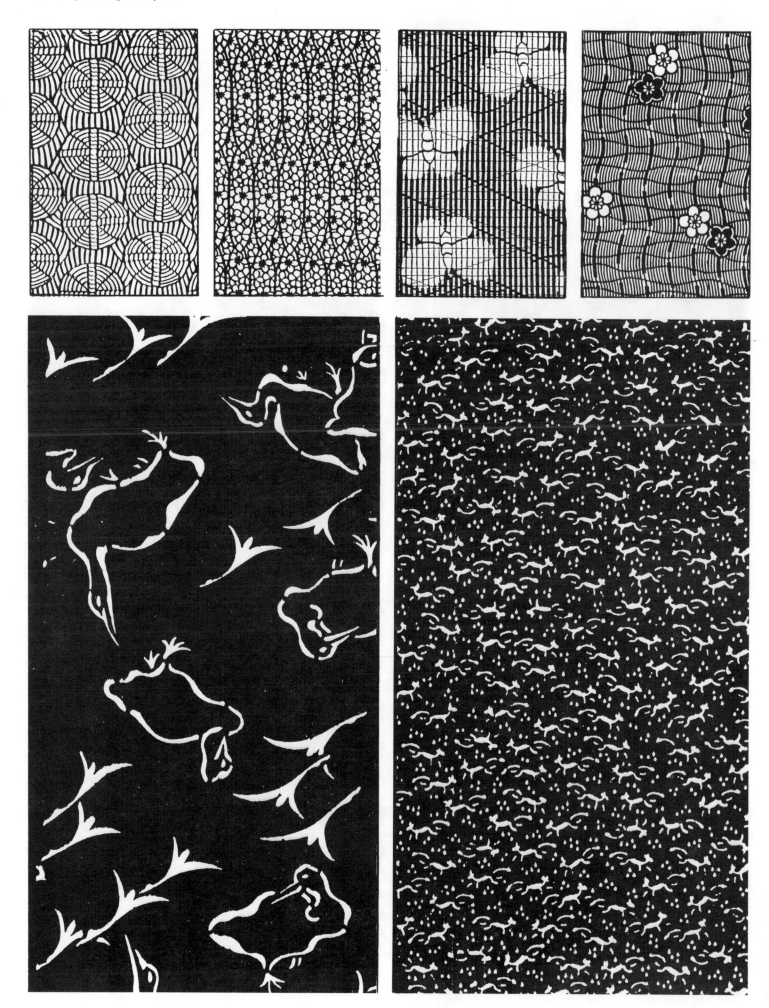

186

This spread
Japanese paper with
stencil cut designs.

This page
Paper-cut patterns.

Above
Paper-cut.

Right
Patterned motif
utilising willow
branches covered in
snow.

Top
Honeysuckle motif
on a lacquer box.

Above middle
Silver and gold
decorative work on a
shrine.

Left
From a decorated
writing paper.

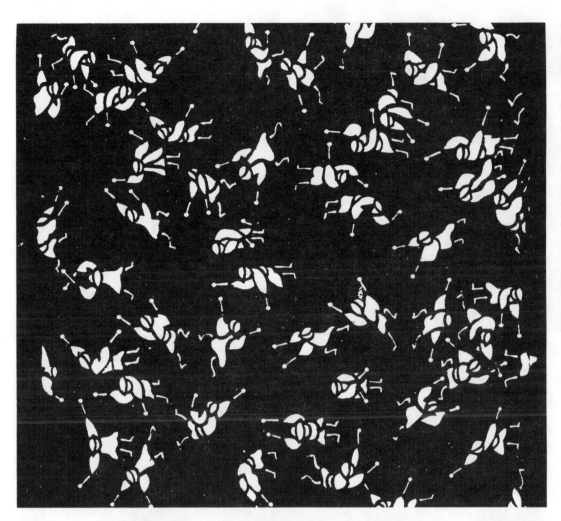

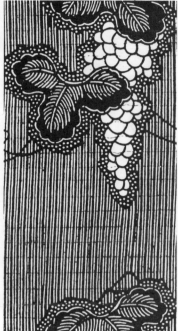

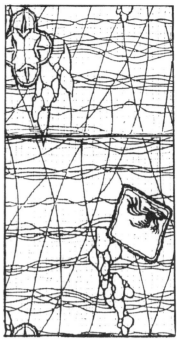

This spread
Japanese paper with
stencil cut designs.

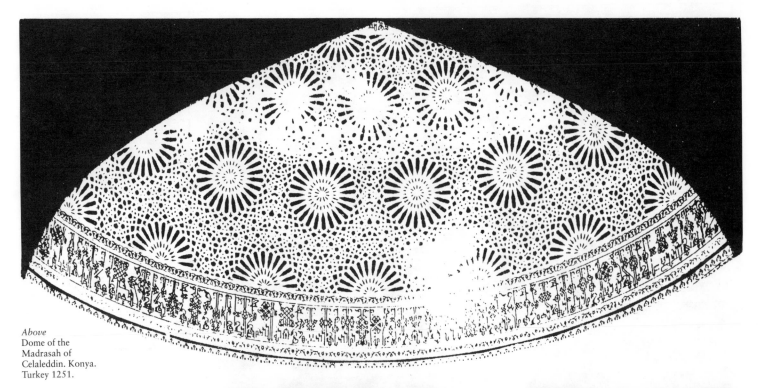

Above
Dome of the
Madrasah of
Celaleddin. Konya.
Turkey 1251.

Above
Mythical birds and
foliated decorations
on an 11th Century
Persian silk cloth.

Right
The calligraphic
emblem of Suleyman
the Magnificent.
16th Century Turkey.

Above right
Calligraphic
peacock.
19th Century
Persian.

Above
Details from the
calligraphic peacock,
(above left).
19th Century Persia.

Near right
From a 14th Century
Koran. Mamluk,
Egypt.

Below
The reverse side of a
jade mirror.
18th Century India.

*Far right top, middle
and lower*
Details from carved
wooden panels.
11th Century Egypt.

Far right bottom
10th Century
Egyptian bowl
showing a boat with
a sail and oars with
fish in the water
beneath.

Above
A representation of Mecca.

Top
Moulds made of clay which were stamped into the dough of unbaked bread. Egypt.

Right
Stylised image of a horseman used to decorate a 10th century plate. Iraq.

Top
A pictographic image of a lion symbolizing strength, constructed from calligraphic words which read "In the name of the lion of God, the face of God, the victorious Ali". From a wall-hanging, Turkey.

Middle left and middle right
The dragon/peacock was a symbol used by the Sasanid inheritance.

Middle centre
The lion and the sun were emblems of Persia in the 13th century.

Far left and left
Two zodiacal signs used as embellishment upon a Persian plate.

Left
Islamic script in its various forms: (top to bottom)
Simple Kufic - simple straight strokes;
Foliated Kufic - the vertical strokes are completed with leaf forms;
Floriated Kufic - the process of foliated and rosette embellishment is further increased;
Naskhi - a cursive form with some of the Kufic foliation retained;
Thuluth - intensified cursive style;
Nastaliq - elegant form with the placement of the elements executed with almost careless ease.

Right
Enamelled brass bowl. Seljuk.

Above
Detail from a bronze vessel. Herat.

Right
Detail of a carpet from the mosque of Alaeddin at Konya. The pattern elements are based on Kufic script.

Left
Central boss from a
brass plate.

Below
Panel from the
Topkapi Sarayi
Museum in Istanbul.

Above
Carved wooden
doors to a
mausoleum.

Right
Ceramic bowl
utilizing the
half-human,
half-animal, sphinx
as its main motif.
Seljuk, Iran.

Below, left
10th century
decorated plaster
panels from
Nishapur, Iran.

Below
10th century bowl
from Nishapur, Iran.

Below
A lectern carved in
wood for a mosque.
13th Century.
Turkey.

Below
Carved lectern.
14th Century
Transoxiana.

Top
Embroidered silk
from Southern Spain.
c.12th Century.

Above
14th Century Nasrid
woven silk from
Southern Spain or
North Africa.

Left
12th Century lustred
bowl. Cairo.

Right
15th Century woven
silk.

This page
A "Garden" carpet
from northwest Iran.
17th Century.

Top left
16th Century velvet cloth decorated with star-shaped flowers. Turkey.

Top middle
Velvet with crescents and flowers. 17th Century Turkey.

Above
Ceramic dish.

Left
Velvet emblazoned with stripes and circles symbolising both the tiger and the leopard. 16th Century Turkey.

Top right
A saddle cloth. 17th Century Turkey.

Right
Velvet cushion cover with central eight-pointed star bordered with star-shaped flowers and tulips. 18th Century Turkey.

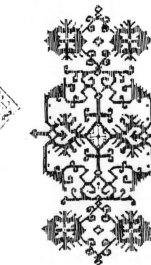

Top left
10th Century
Persian dish.

Top
13th Century
book binding.

*Above, left and
above*
Details from carpets.

Left and right
Open metalwork.

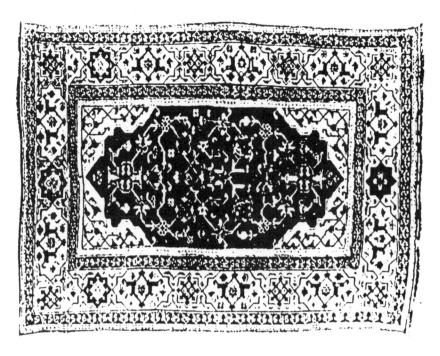

Above
12th Century Persian
lustre dish.

Above and right
So-called
Transylvanian rugs.
17th Century
Anatolia.

Below
17th Century Ushak
rug.

Above
Detail from a woven
carpet.

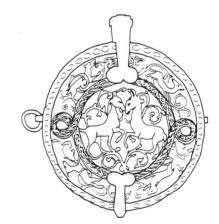

Right
Detail of ivory
carving.

Above
Ceramic decoration
to a 16th Century
plate.

Above top
Tile of the Seljuk
culture. Anatolia.
11th Century.

Above
Head of a Turkish
battle standard.

Above
Persian plate.
16th Century.

Right
Painted leather
template for
Egyptian shadow-
plays.

Above
From a lustre dish.
Persia, 12th Century.

Above right
Ewer motif, in
several variants,
from tiles in Tawrizi,
Damascus and Cairo.

Above
10th Century dish
from Nishapur,
Persia.

Left
Painted bowl.
Nishapur..
10th Century.

Above
A leaf motif on a
14th Century
Chinese dish.

205

This page
Square tiles from the
Arab Museum in
Cairo.

Above
Mamluk heraldic
devices.

Above
Like most medieval
maps this is largely
schematic and only
incidentally
indicative of the
geographical features
it represents. The
incursion on the left
is the Mediterranean
and that on the right
is the Red Sea.
Baghdad.
14th Century.

Right
Late Mamluk
heraldic bearing
from a stone relief.
Aleppo.

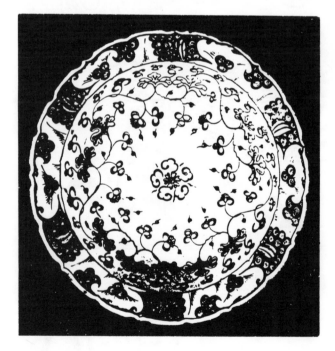

Above
16th Century
Iznik plate.

Right above
Two examples of
16th Century
decorated Iznik
ceramic ware.

Above
Mid-16th Century
Iznik plate.

Right
Early 16th Century
Iznik plate.

Right
12th Century lustred
plate.

Left
Early 17th Century
Iznik plate.

Right
Ceramic bowl from
Iraq.

Left
Peacock on 9th
Century Persian
bowl.

Below left
Bowl decorated with
bird motif and
imitation script.
10th Century
Nishapur.

Below
Lion and Sun from a
banner.
19th Century Persia.

Top left
Rug.
15th Century Turkey.

Left middle
Bowl painted with
the inscription
"Complete favor and
perfect blessing".
11th Century Egypt.

Left lower
Bowl decorated with
cheetahs.
11th Century Egypt.

Left bottom
10th Century bowl
from Transoxiana.

Right
Peacock decorating
9th Century Persian
bowl.

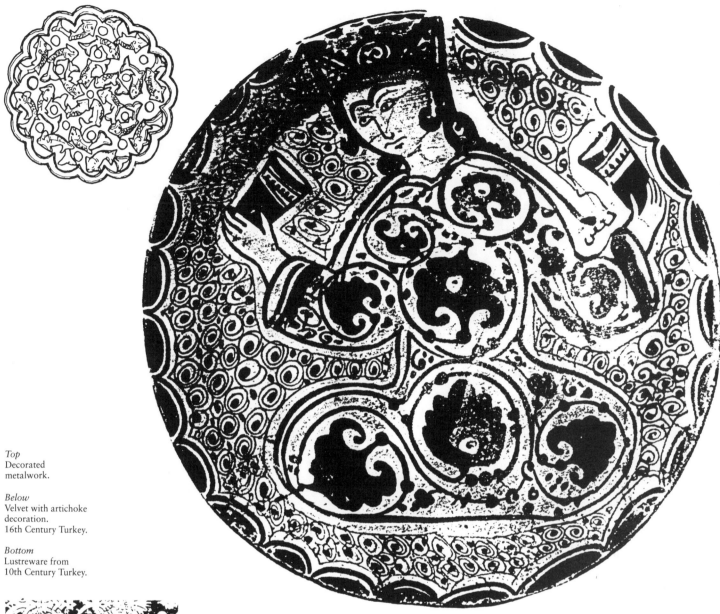

Top
Decorated
metalwork.

Below
Velvet with artichoke
decoration.
16th Century Turkey.

Bottom
Lustreware from
10th Century Turkey.

Top
Seated woman or
young man holding
beakers.
11th Century Egypt.

Above
Manuscript carrying
a blessing to
Muhammad.
19th Century Persia.

Right
Detail from a
beaten-brass ewer.
Mesopotamia.

211

Top
Persian dish.

Above
10th Century bowl.
Eastern Persia.

Above right
Cover embroidered
with stylized dragon.
18th Century
Caucasus.

Top far right
Velvet decorated
with carnations and
tulips.
16th Century Turkey.

Far right bottom
14th Century
Mamluk miniature.

Right
Animal motif on
12th Century Persian
dish.

Above
Winged mythical
beast on 12th
Century Persian dish.

Right
13th Century Persian
tiles.

Left
16th Century
Turkish jug.

Left
17th Century
Turkish carpet with
bird and leaf
decoration.

Above
13th Century Persian
tile.

213

This spread
Tile patterns from
the mosque of
Murad II, Edirne.
15th Century.

This spread
Tile patterns from
the 15th Century
mosque of Murad II,
Edirne and from the
tomb of Ghars
ad-Din al-Khalil
at-Tawrizi,
Damascus.

Left and opposite page
Tiles from the tomb
of Ghars ad-Din
al-Khalil at-Tawrizi,
Damascus
and from the Arab
Museum in Cairo.

Above
Tiles in the
Kataeesh mosque,
Sidon.

219

Top
The Mexican Sun
God.

Above
Woodcut showing a
sundial with
horizontal
projection.
16th Century.

Right top
Printer's mark.

Right middle
Title page. Germany,
late 15th Century.

Right
Woodcut from
Switzerland.
15th Century.

Il Secolo Messicano.

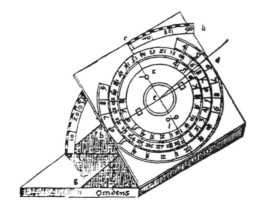

Above
Engraving in copper
from an Italian
history of Mexico.
18th Century.

Far right
Motif drawn by the
17th Century English
calligrapher, Edward
Cocker.

Near right
Woodcut of 16th
Century sundial.

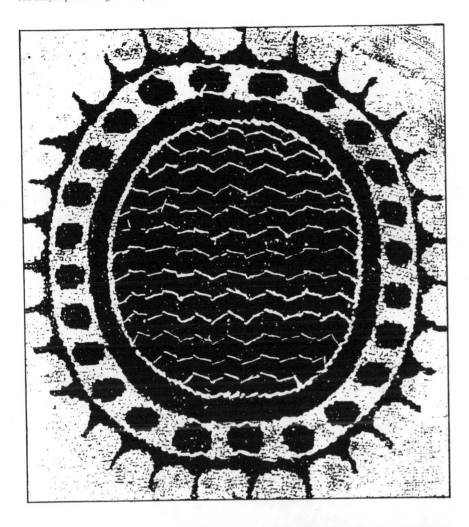

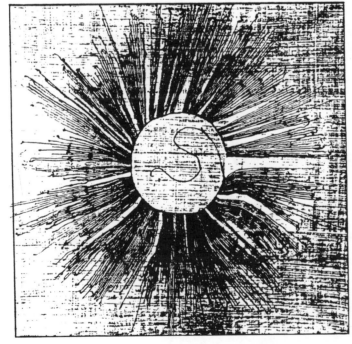

Left
The Sun united with
the Sea. From a
Coptic fabric.

Below
An Italian
trademark.

Above
The image of the Sun
used as a calendar.
This Peruvian device
uses the rays of the
sun as a record of the
days. The twisting
curve in the centre
records its
movement.

Right above
Mesopotamia,
13th Century.

Right
The Sun and the
Lion. A royal device
of Persian sultans.

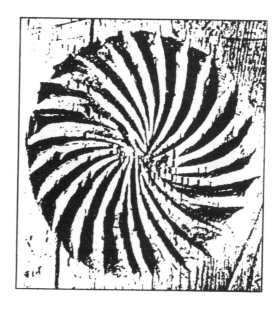

Top left
The Sun carrying a
bag of incense and
instruments of
penitence.

Top right
German calendar.

Middle
Chart with a graphic
display of solar
eclipses.

Far left
German,
17th Century.

Left
Wood engraving.

223

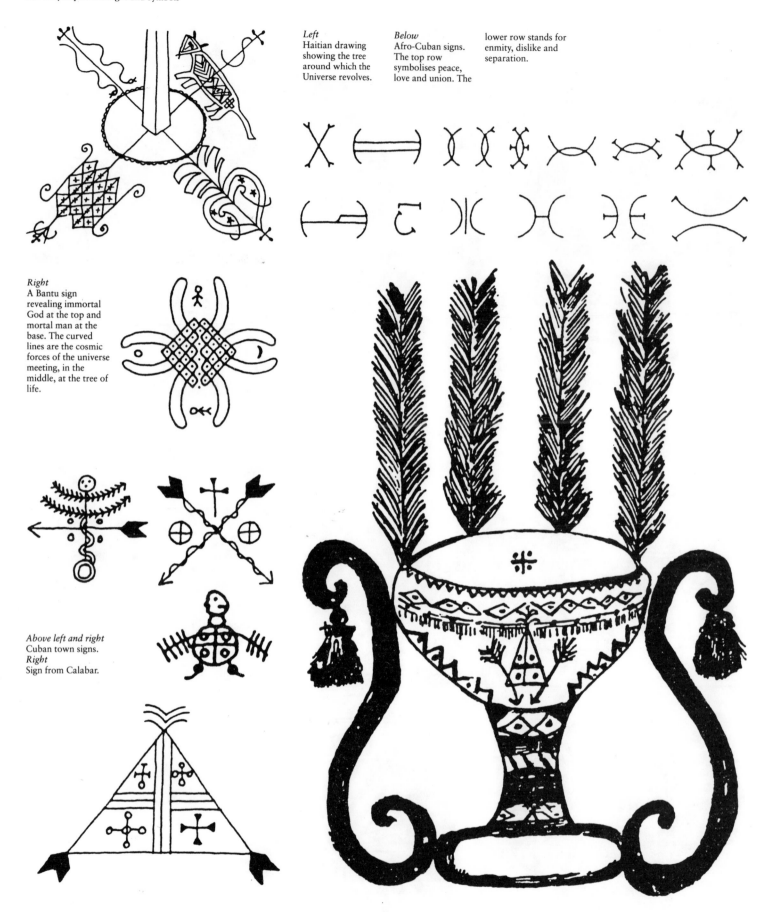

Left
Haitian drawing showing the tree around which the Universe revolves.

Below
Afro-Cuban signs. The top row symbolises peace, love and union. The lower row stands for enmity, dislike and separation.

Right
A Bantu sign revealing immortal God at the top and mortal man at the base. The curved lines are the cosmic forces of the universe meeting, in the middle, at the tree of life.

Above left and right
Cuban town signs.
Right
Sign from Calabar.

Above
A Cuban sign from Havana in the 19th Century symbolising hostility and loss of life.

Above
The Cuban sign for a drum that is to be heard in contemplation, not in actuality.

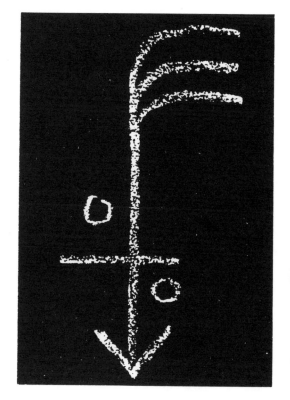

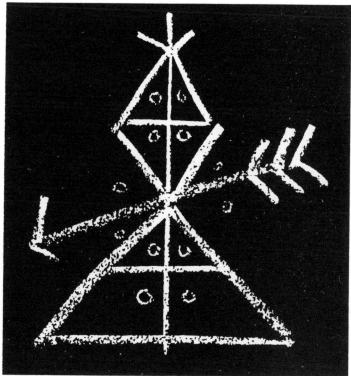

Far left
The arrow divides the two worlds and symbolizes death and loss.

Left
The vigilance of threatening forces.

Left
The gods watch and survey the progression of creation.

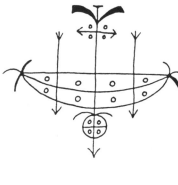

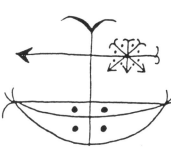

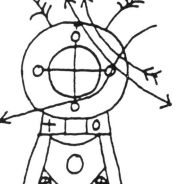

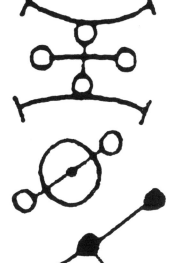

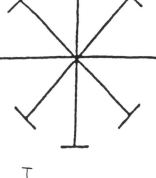

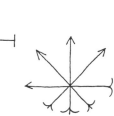

Above top
A reminder that the ancients are forever vigilant.

Above
A sign giving the subject the authority to assume a position within society.

Above top
A war and blood sign from Cuba.

Above
Sign accompanying the telling of a story.

Above
Three signs indicating, top, two people having an argument, middle, a wound and, at the bottom, a bow with a poisoned arrow.

Above
Three signs indicating speech and the power of spiritual attack.

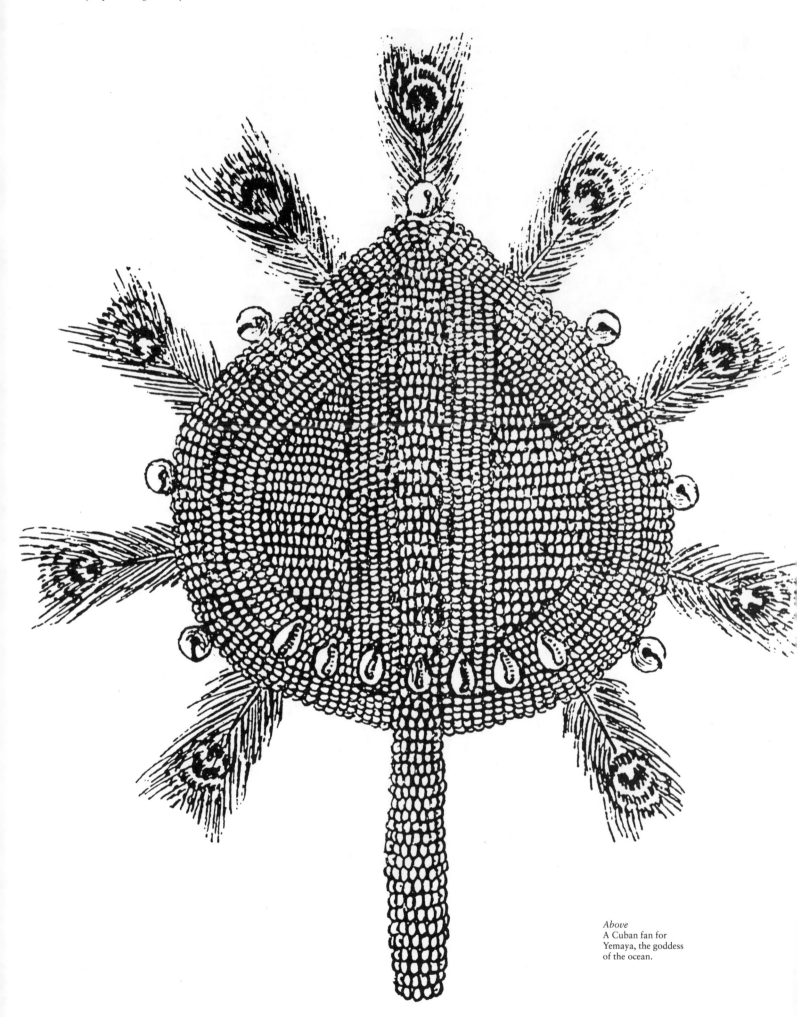

Above
A Cuban fan for
Yemaya, the goddess
of the ocean.

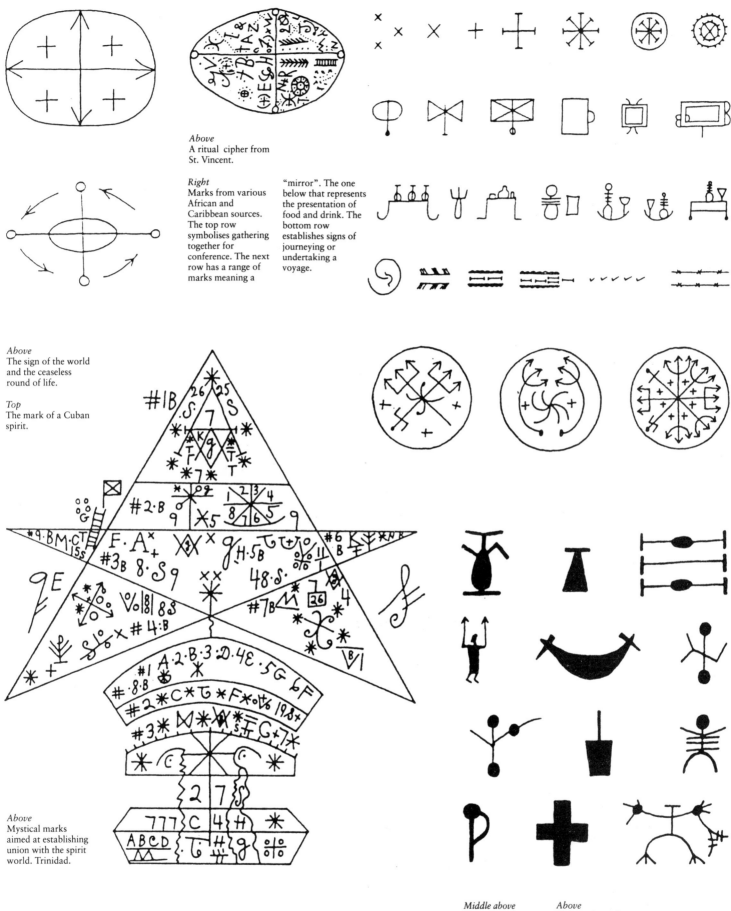

Above
A ritual cipher from St. Vincent.

Right
Marks from various African and Caribbean sources. The top row symbolises gathering together for conference. The next row has a range of marks meaning a "mirror". The one below that represents the presentation of food and drink. The bottom row establishes signs of journeying or undertaking a voyage.

Above
The sign of the world and the ceaseless round of life.

Top
The mark of a Cuban spirit.

Above
Mystical marks aimed at establishing union with the spirit world. Trinidad.

Middle above
These three signs represent the Yoruba god of evil, Eshu and his influence over unpredictable changes of fortune.

Above
Various signs of warning or danger found in Afro-Caribbean societies.

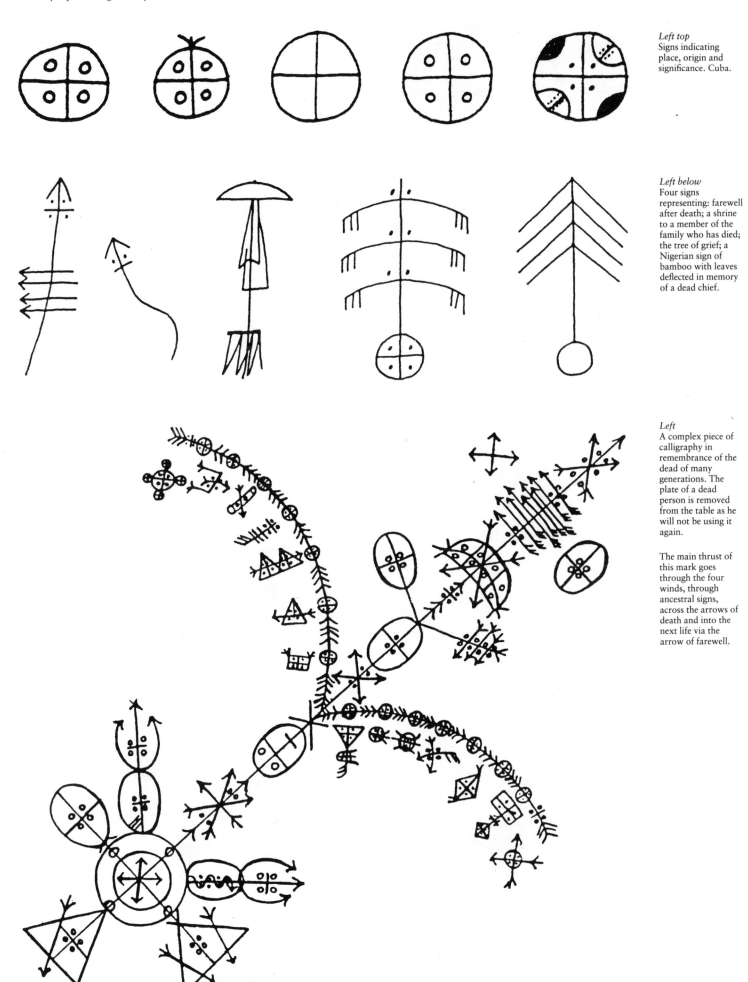

Left top
Signs indicating place, origin and significance. Cuba.

Left below
Four signs representing: farewell after death; a shrine to a member of the family who has died; the tree of grief; a Nigerian sign of bamboo with leaves deflected in memory of a dead chief.

Left
A complex piece of calligraphy in remembrance of the dead of many generations. The plate of a dead person is removed from the table as he will not be using it again.

The main thrust of this mark goes through the four winds, through ancestral signs, across the arrows of death and into the next life via the arrow of farewell.

228

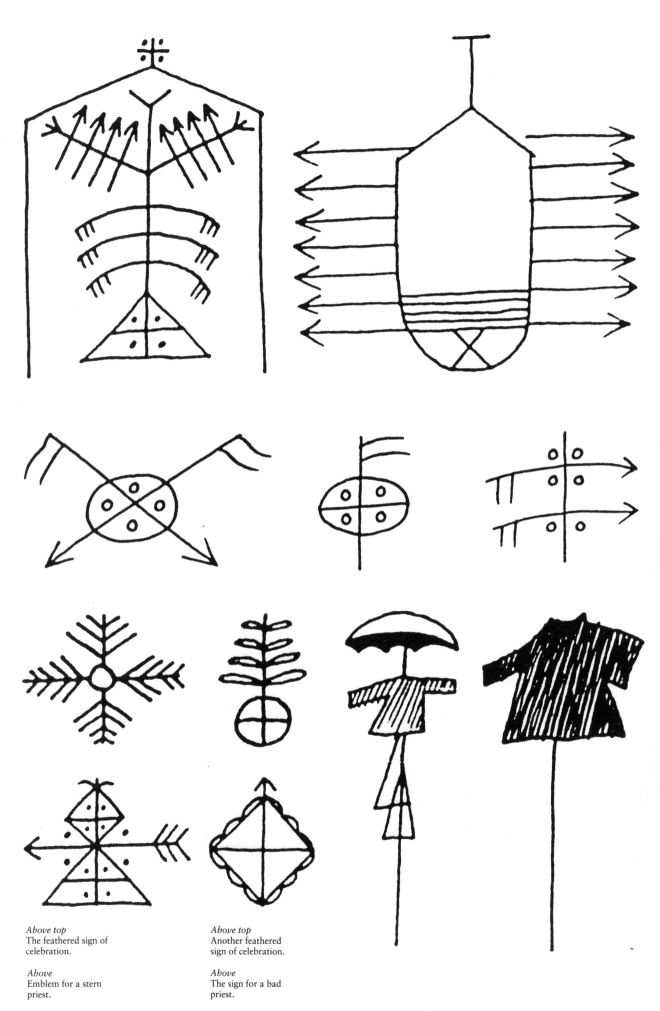

Far left
Funeral flag.

Left
The seven spears used by a murdering father and the seven spears used by his son in defence.

Left
The use of a damaged, feathered arrow signify aspects of death.

Above top
The feathered sign of celebration.

Above
Emblem for a stern priest.

Above top
Another feathered sign of celebration.

Above
The sign for a bad priest.

Far left and left
The arrow held with its point upwards signifies the rising of the spirit to heaven. These marks recall the habit in Nigeria of putting clothes at the top of trees to mark the progression of an important personage from this world to the superior one beyond.

229

Far left
The eye of God.

Left
The eyes of dead
ancestors.
Both 16th Century.

Right
Figure with a head
which is both the Sun
and an eye.
Algonquin rock
engraving.

Left
The God who
threatens those
foolish enough to
drink too much
intoxicating liquor.

Above
The creation of the
first action.
17th Century.

Right
The Lamb of God
with seven eyes. The
number seven is
accorded great
power in many
cultures. Christian,
13th Century.

Near right
Three lines together symbolise power and in this Transylvanian dish are associated with a whirling spiral of energy.

Middle right
Here the three lines are associated with seed-pods, the producers of life.

Far right
The association of a moon's phase with the three line motif here produces a dazzling jostle of movement.

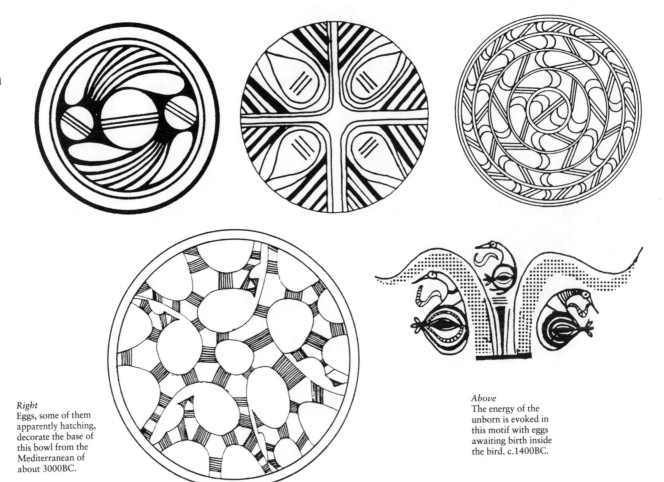

Right
Eggs, some of them apparently hatching, decorate the base of this bowl from the Mediterranean of about 3000BC.

Above
The energy of the unborn is evoked in this motif with eggs awaiting birth inside the bird. c.1400BC.

The imprint of man, or possibly a god, is established by placing his footprints amongst images of ships and snakes. From an ancient rock engraving in Sweden.

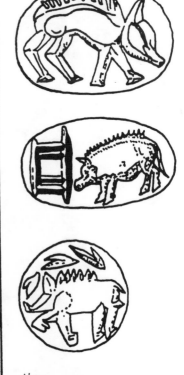

Above
Three images of the wild boar from Minoan culture c.1800BC.

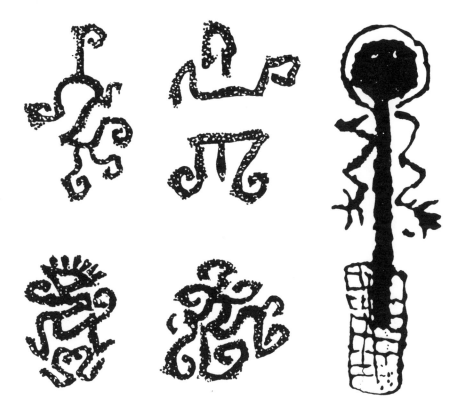

Left and below
The association of snake forms with those of human or god/goddess images occur in various parts of the Mediterranean around 5000BC.

Near right
This three part compound is of Celtic origin.

Far right
Magic squares are common to many cultures. This one, known as the square of Saturn, is based on the number 5. Additions and subtractions on all lines lead to the number five or one of its multiples.

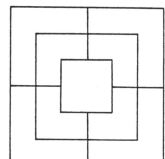

8	1	6
3	5	7
4	9	2

Right
The union of opposites features in all mythologies. Fire and water are juxtaposed in this Aztec pictogram.

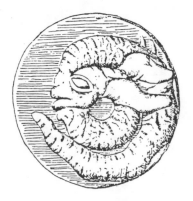

Left
Two Bohemian coins
bearing the image of
a dragon. c.100BC.

Above
The transformational
steps in the creation
of a woman from a
tree. 17th Century,
France.

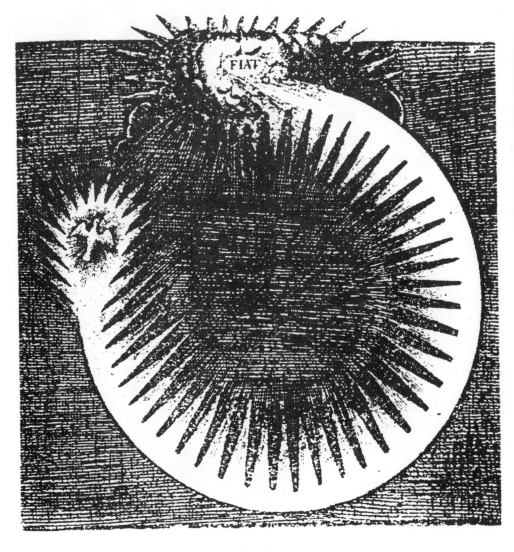

Left
God's Word leads to
the creation of the
world. Robert Fludd,

Above
An image of the
gorgon with hair of
snakes. c.500BC.

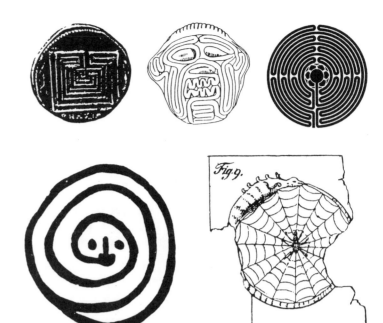

Far left top
A man guilty of sexual infidelity is condemned after death to have his soul trapped with a stamping mule.

Above top
From right to left: a Trojan Labyrinth; the intestinal Babylonian God, Humbaba; a maze from Chartres Cathedral.

Above left
A serpent in the form of a maze from a cave in Italy.

Above right
The spider's web forms a Brahmin maze.

Left
The snake of the Marinbata tribe in Arnhem Land.

Below
A shaman is despatched to retrieve the soul of a friend from the Tree of Life.

Left
A mixture of man, ram and bird. Mediterranean around 1500BC.

Above
An aboriginal bark painting showing the path of the dead.

Top
The Lightning Spirit as shown on an aboriginal bark painting.

Above
Another bark painting shows two women being swallowed by the Serpent of the Rainbow.

Below
Christ revealing the
Four Elements to the
world. 15th Century.

Right
A German
Cabbalistic image of
the Hand of God.
17th Century.

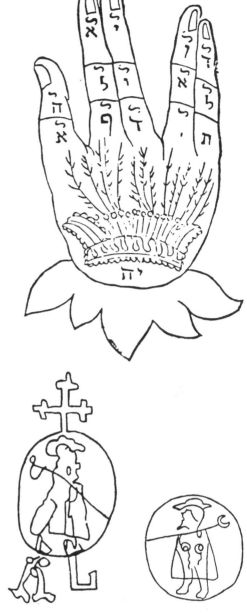

Below
Three Shang dynasty
inscriptions:
at left, a man and his
grandson offer meat
to an ancestor figure;
middle, an ancestor

shows his thanks by
leaving behind him
his footprints; at
right, the ancestor
watches the
sacrificial victim.

Right
A mythical figure,
with a Christian
cross.

Far right
The man in the moon
carries her at the end
of his staff.

Both these images are
taken from
watermarks.

Above
A Romanian ceramic
reveals the snake
with the eyes of
truth.

Right
Eyes also feature on
two pots, in
combination with
motifs associated
with the moon and
with the ram.

Above
A Huichol painting
of the Grandmother
Goddess holding
within her the bird
who is the protector
of the maize. The sun
and the rain, above
her head, nourish the
crops.

Above
Sea Goddess feeding
her young.

Right
Birth with its
attendants and the
father enclosed.

Left
Gods with the eyes
from which none can
escape.

Above
The Tree of the Sun.
Greece c.800BC.

Below
The Gorgon.

239

Above
A drawing of a Malaysian dreaming inside the hut of a shaman. The central dot is the dreamer; the spokes of the image are the leaves which form the roof of the hut and the outer circle is the rim of the hut and, by extension, the circumference of the world. The five sections of the circle represent the five aspects of a human soul.

Below
The husband of a female shaman and their helpers in the spiritual world.

Above
A painting of a dream had by a shaman who had married two women who did not agree. In his dream they lived harmoniously in a large house which he recorded in this image.

Left
The dreamer approaches spiritual fulfilment by awakening the five organs of perception. Iran. 16th Century.

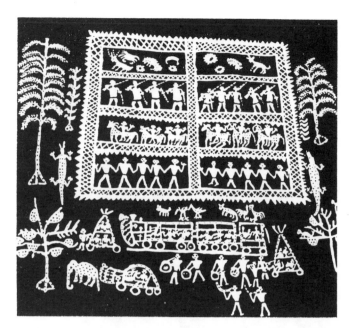

Top
A picture painted to comfort a dead husband who had threatened crop failure unless his wife made a painting recording his spirit life.

Middle
A picture showing the harmony between shamans and their spirtual colleagues.

Left
The image of a scorpion, in Tibet, protects a person from evil forces met in dreams.

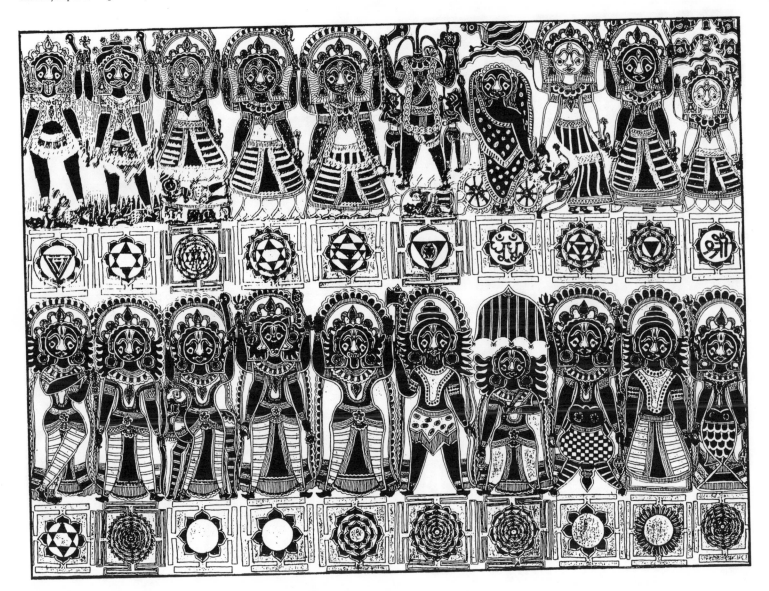

Top
The goddess appears
in many forms,
representing the dark
and the light sides of
existence. Only in
contrast can life be
said to have any
meaning. India.

Above
Shamanic figures of
man united with the
deer occur in many
cultures. These three
are from France and
Spain and date from
around 12,000BC.

Above
Snakes in dual form
and a sea creature
appear on Minoan
seals of c.2000BC.

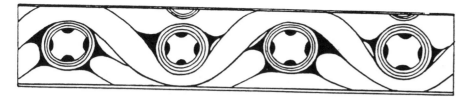

Left
Snakes wind themselves around eggs or the world. c.3800BC eastern Europe.

Above
The snake is here surrounded by the powerful three line motif.
Minoa c.2000BC.

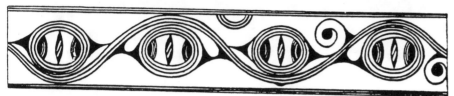

Left
The Goddess associates with all of life and in this Saharan wall painting runs through nature.

Above
A Pictish Goddess with hair and lower limbs as snakes. Early AD.

Above
A Greek vase of c.700BC depicts the horns of a ram.

Left
A house of the spiritual world is attended by human acolytes. From a pre-historic rock carving in Italy.

Opposite page
This segmented
wheel from a Tibetan
monastery indicates
the misleading
evidence of the
material world which
has to be
circumvented before
reaching the subtler
truths of the dream
world.

Right
A Chukchi map of
the journey to be
made by the human
soul from the
internal world,
through the earth to
the ultimate spirit
world.

Right
A dream artifact; the
retention of a strong
image experienced in
a dream,
subsequently used
for guidance in the
waking life.

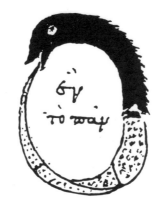

Left
According to the
alchemists the image
of a snake
swallowing its tail
was symbolic of
creative energy.
The German chemist
August von Kekulé
claimed that the
structure of the ring
molecule of benzene
came to him in a
dream of a serpent
swallowing its tail.

Above left and above
The Saora tribe in
India receive
communications
from the spritual
world through
dreams which are
then painted on the
walls of their houses.

LA FORCE

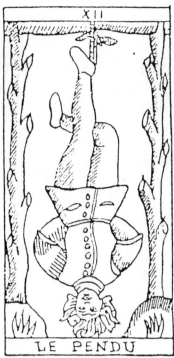

LE PENDU

LE · DIABLE

TEMPERANCE

Top
La Force:
The domination of
matter by the mind.

Above
Death:
The symbol of
relentless movement
which exacts the
demands of fate, as
corn is reaped by the
scythe.

Top
The Hanged Man:
That which is up can
also look the same as
that which is down.
We are bound by fate
and lack free will.

Above
Temperance:
Nothing should be
done too abruptly.

Above
The Devil:
Triumph achieved by
scheming and
fraudulent means. It
promises
punishment, as gains
made by trickery can
only be temporary in
their effect.

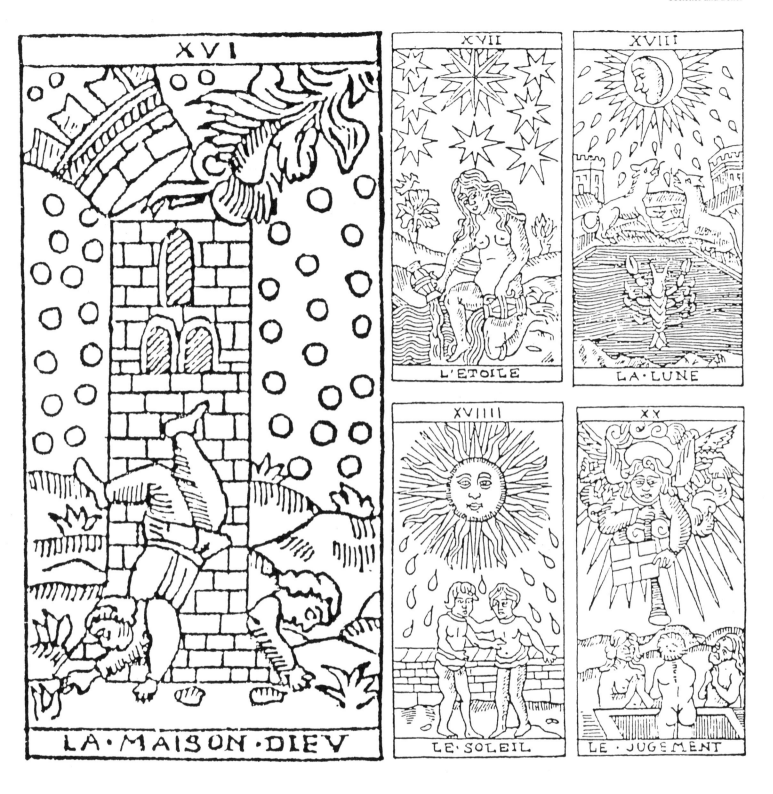

Above
The Tower of
Destruction:
The imaginary
creations produced
in the mind through
desire and which
have a tendency to be
brought to an abrupt
halt!

Top
The Star:
Harmony based on
any form of the
psychic or spiritual.

Above
The Sun:
All-embracing
radiance. Triumph
and success
irregardless of
circumstance.

Top
The Moon:
Illusion arising
through scandal, or
the revelation of a
secret.

Above
Judgement:
The call to achieve a
higher state of being
transcending the
mere physical plane.

Far left
6th Century carved
eagle.

Left
The Lion of St.Mark
from the Book of
Durrow. Dublin.

Above
The Signs of the
Zodiac as inlaid in
the 13th Century
church of San
Miniato in Florence.

Above
An eagle from the
8th Century Dimma
manuscript. Dublin.

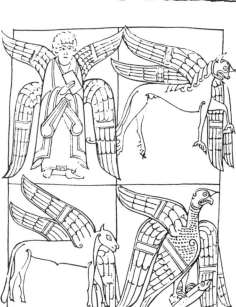

Left
The four Evangelists
from the Book of
Armagh, 9th
Century. Dublin.

Above
Swiss image of the
fish with the Host .

Above
Stone seal.

Below
Three fishes form a
roof boss in Bristol
Cathedral.

Bottom
6th Century Coptic
stone carving of a
dolphin with the
Cross and the Vine.

Above left
An 8th Century
carving of the ox of
St.Luke.

Above right
The eagle of St.John.
8th Century.

Left
An 11th Century
winged eagle from a
Durham bible.

Above
7th Century beaked
griffin. Byzantine.

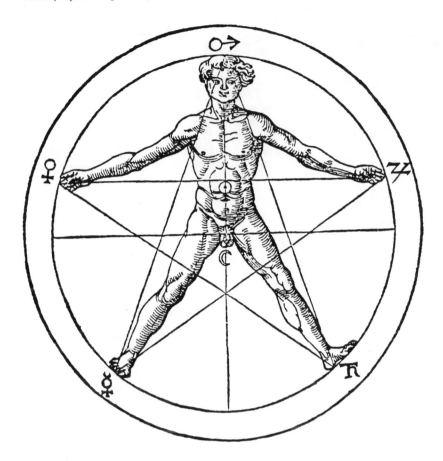

Left
A Vitruvian figure by Agrippa in the form of a pentangle.

Below
Other Vitruvian figures, from left to right: by Giorgio to illustrate the "Exempada"; conforming to a square configuration; relating to the signs of the Zodiac; matching St. Andrew's Cross; relating to the planetary signs.

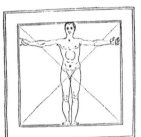
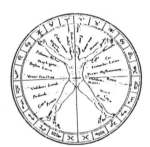
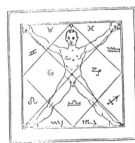

Above
The Philistine God, Dagon.

Above
From "The Book of Angels", an amulet based on the hexagrammatical Shield of Solomon.

Right
The Grand Pentacle of Solomon which can summon or banish spirits.

250

Below
Beneath "The Watchful Eye" and accompanied by the Serpent, the Word and the Staff stands another Vitruvian figure.

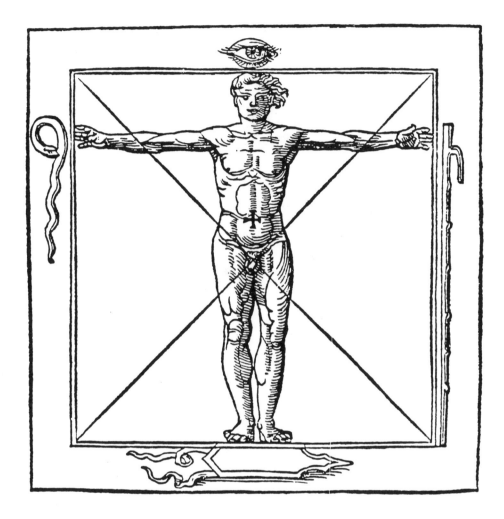

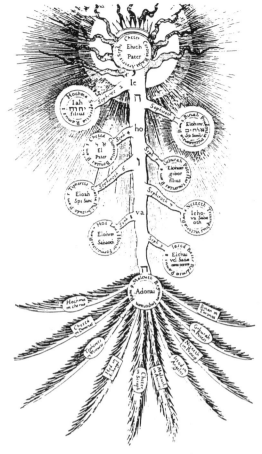

Bottom
On a white horse Gabriel spears the evil eye in the form of a devil woman.

Top
The Sephirotic Tree from "Philosophia Sacra" by Robert Fludd, a 17th Century book printed in Germany.

Above
Belial dancing for King Solomon.

251

Right
36 of the 72 Hebrew names of God.

Above
This sign was reputed to bring about the falling of the stars from the sky.

Sunday	Monday	Tuesday	Wednesday	Thursday	Friday	Saturday
Michaël	Gabriel	Camael	Raphaël	Sachiel	Anaël	Caffiel
☉ ♌	☽ ♋	♈ ♂ ♏	♊ ♍	♐ ♓	♉ ♎	♑ ♒
name of the 4 Heaven	name of the 1 Heaven	name of the 5 Heaven	name of the 2 Heaven	name of the 6 Heaven	name of the 3 Heaven	9: Angels ruling above the 6 Heaven
Machen.	Shamain.	Machon.	Raquie.	Zebul.	Sagun.	

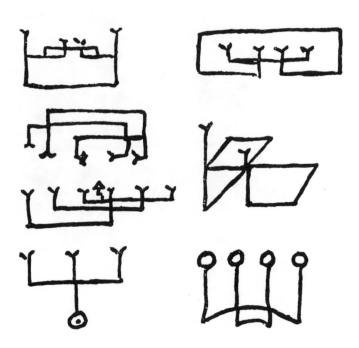

Above
The imprint of the Power Angels.

Above right
The names of the Angels who command each day of the week.

Right
The Seals of the Seven Angels who between them have the powers of War, Alchemy, Magic, the Physical World, the Moon, the Seas and all Precious Metals. In addition they had control over 133,000 legions of spirits and command of 17,640,000 individual spirits.

Left
The remaining 36 0f the 72 names of God taken from "The Sixth and the Seventh Books of Moses".

Left
The remaining 36 0f the 72 names of God taken from "The Sixth and the Seventh Books of Moses".

Right
Characters which go to form The Angelic Script.

Left
The "Triumph of Death" with Angels, Seraphim and Devils fighting for the souls of the dead. In the Campo Santo, Pisa.

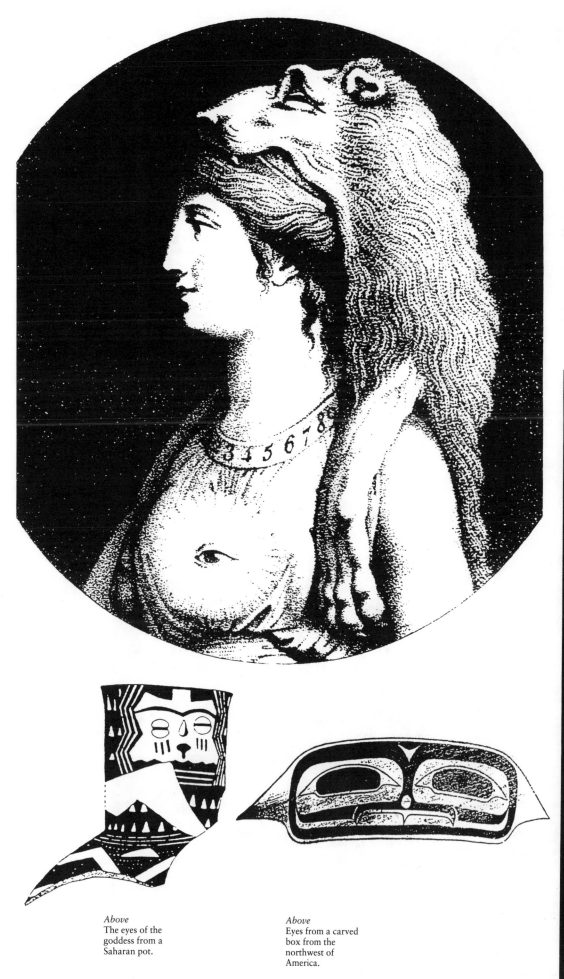

Left
An engraving from the time of the French Revolution. The eye of Truth shines from the breast of Reason. The numbers around her neck further emphasise the rational control that was to be brought about by the new order.

Below
The face is the most powerful image and can convey love, kinship and fear. Two war shields from Borneo.

Above
The eyes of the goddess from a Saharan pot.

Above
Eyes from a carved box from the northwest of America.

The letters Chi and Rho, rendered in writing as P and X, form the first two letters of Christ's name in Greek. Over the centuries this has formed many images of the Cross and, hence, of Christian significance.

The association of Christianity with the image of the fish can be seen in the image immediately above. It stems from taking the letters of the Greek word for "fish", i.ch.th.u.s., which can stand for Jesus(i) Christ(ch) God's(th) Son(u) Saviour(s).

Above
An American Indian mask of the blind goddess of Fate who eats children and imposes bad dreams.

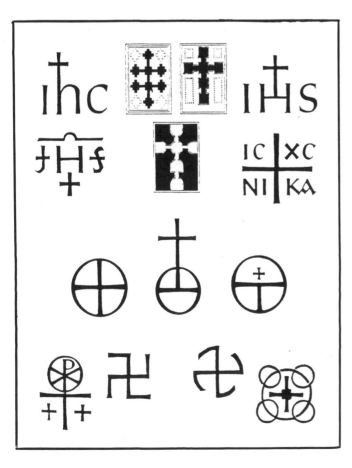

Far left
Various Christian monograms. The swastika, despite its unacceptable 20th century associations, was originally a combination of the cross motif with that of the wheel or the orb of the sun.

Above
From the Book of Kells. 8th Century.

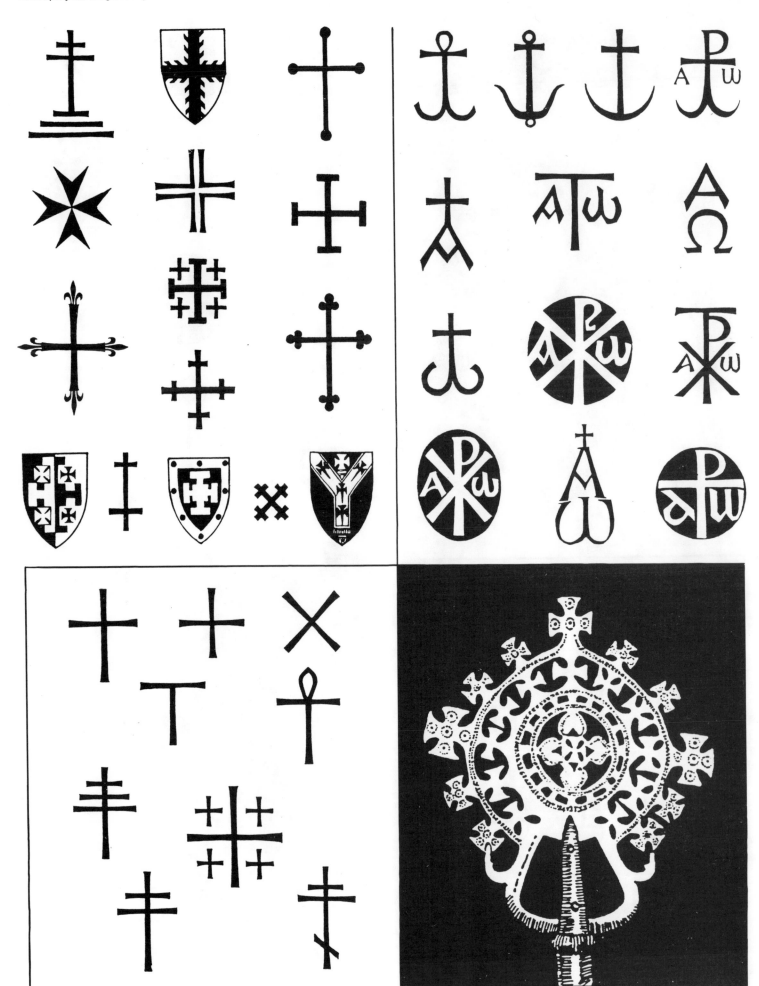

Top left
The Well of Life.

Top middle
A form of the Cross
once used to enable
exorcism.
12th Century.

Far and middle left
Heraldic devices
associated with
St.James of
Compostella.

Left
The winged ox,
which was the
symbol of St.Luke.
12th Century.

Below
The symbol of
St.Luke from an 11th
Century bible.
Durham.

Above
The winged lion of
St.Mark.
14th Century.

*Opposite page top
left*
The Cross in
heraldry.

*Opposite page top
right*
The Cross linked
with the anchor,
alpha and omega as
the beginning and
the end, and the

cross linked with the
letter tau.

Opposite bottom left
Further forms of the
Cross.

Above
Various crosses in
metal.

Opposite bottom
An Abyssinian cross
of brass.

257

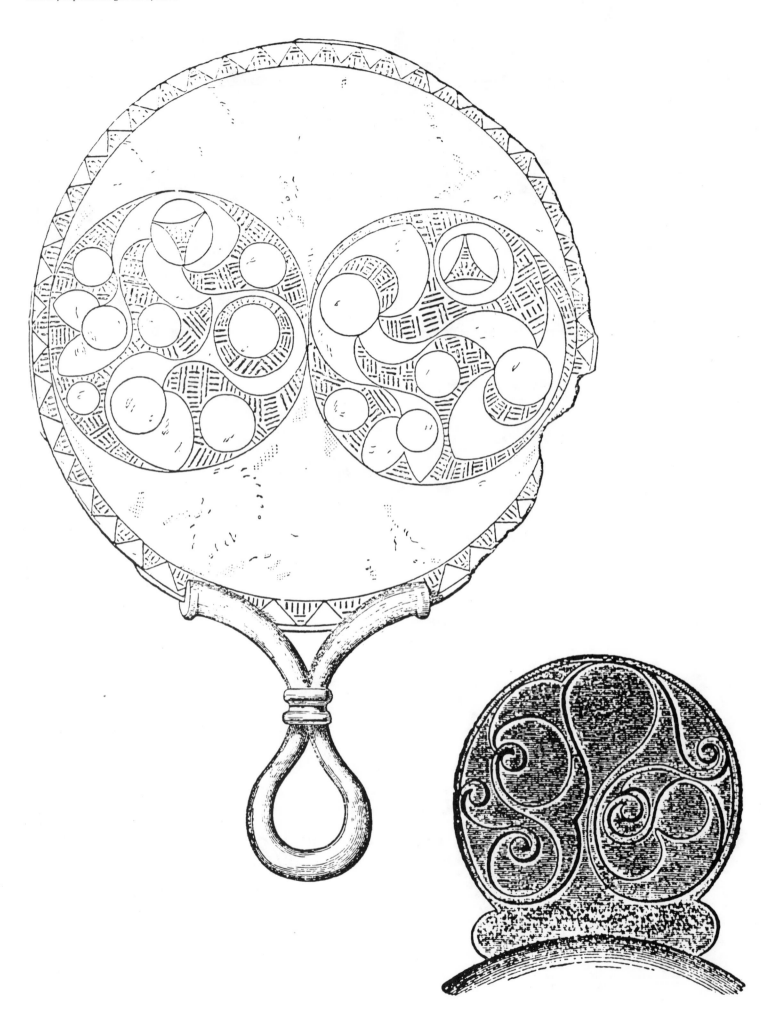

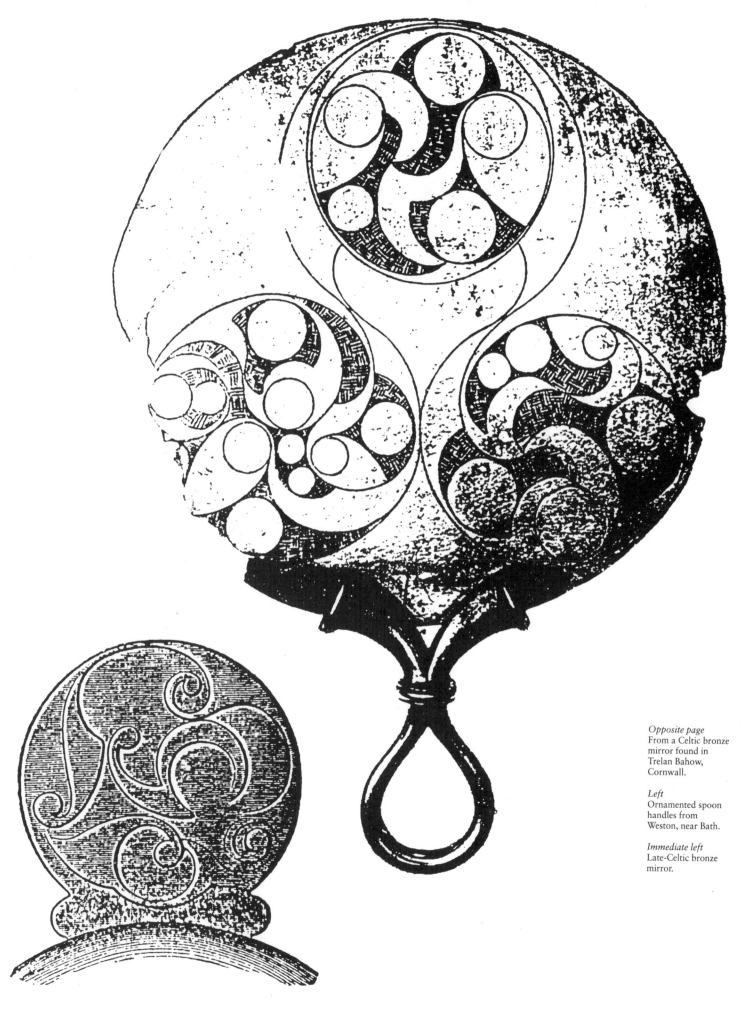

Opposite page
From a Celtic bronze mirror found in Trelan Bahow, Cornwall.

Left
Ornamented spoon handles from Weston, near Bath.

Immediate left
Late-Celtic bronze mirror.

Top left
A spiral ornament,
Book of Kells.

Top right
A winding band
taking the form of a
curved swastika,
sculpted in rock near
Ilkley in Yorkshire.

Above
Swastika design
found on a shield
recovered from the
River Thames.

Right
A bronze bowl from
Chesterton-on-
Fossway in
Warwickshire.

Left
Pierced marble
screen, Ravenna.

Above
Interconnecting
spiral motif.

Top
Key pattern from the
Church of San
Apollinare in
Ravenna.

Above
Spiral ornament
from an illuminated
manuscript.

Right
Cup and ring rock
carving from Ilkley
in Yorkshire.

261

Right
Triangular knot-work from Dunfallandy in Perthshire.

Below
Key patterns from Haddington, Linlithgow, Fife and Sutherland.

262

Right
Four men forming a
swastika from
Meigle in Perthshire.

Below
Four key patterns
from Ross Shire,
Sutherland,
Roxburgh and Ross.

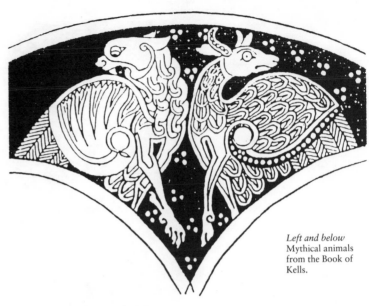

Left and below
Mythical animals
from the Book of
Kells.

Above
A design by
Leonardo da Vinci as
a basis for the work
of a craftsman.

Below
From the Book of
Kells.

From the Book of
Kells:
Above left
Man with his head in
a beast's mouth.
Above
Convoluted beast.
Left
Two beasts.
Below left
Two interlocking
creatures.

Above
Stone carving from
Perthshire.
Left
Two entwined figures
from the Book of
Kells.

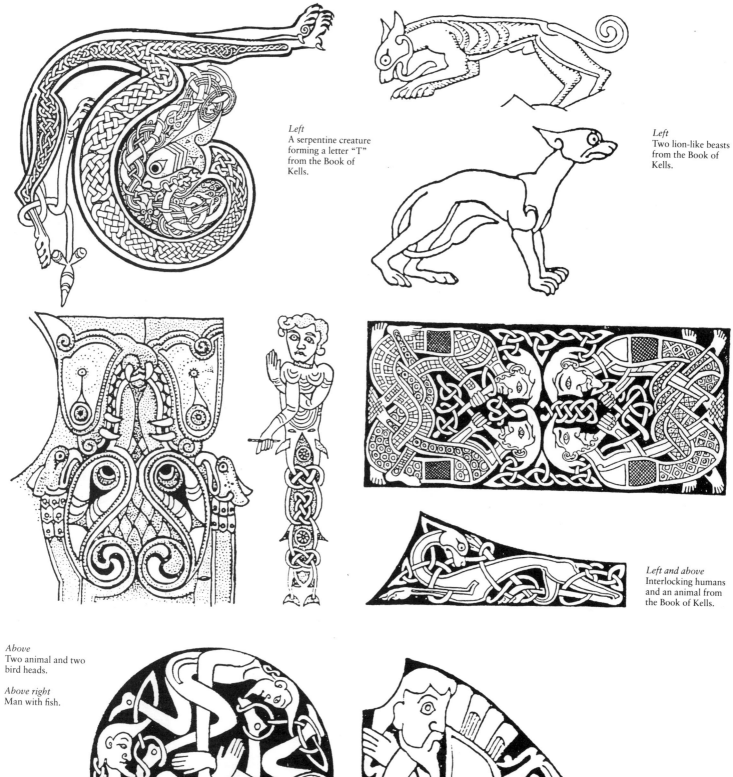

Left
A serpentine creature forming a letter "T" from the Book of Kells.

Left
Two lion-like beasts from the Book of Kells.

Left and above
Interlocking humans and an animal from the Book of Kells.

Above
Two animal and two bird heads.

Above right
Man with fish.

Right
Three entwined men from the Book of Kells.

Left
A man and a bird entwined, from the Book of Kells.

Far left
Stone carved motif from Clanmacnoise in Ireland.

Left
Interlaced animals from the Book of Kells.

Right
Interweaving birds.

Far left
Two dogs.

Left
Entwined reptiles.

Far left
Spirals from the Book of Durrow.

Left
Knotted reptiles from the Book of Kells.

Left
Six birds.

Far left
Spiral work from the Book of Kells.

Left
Six interlaced birds.

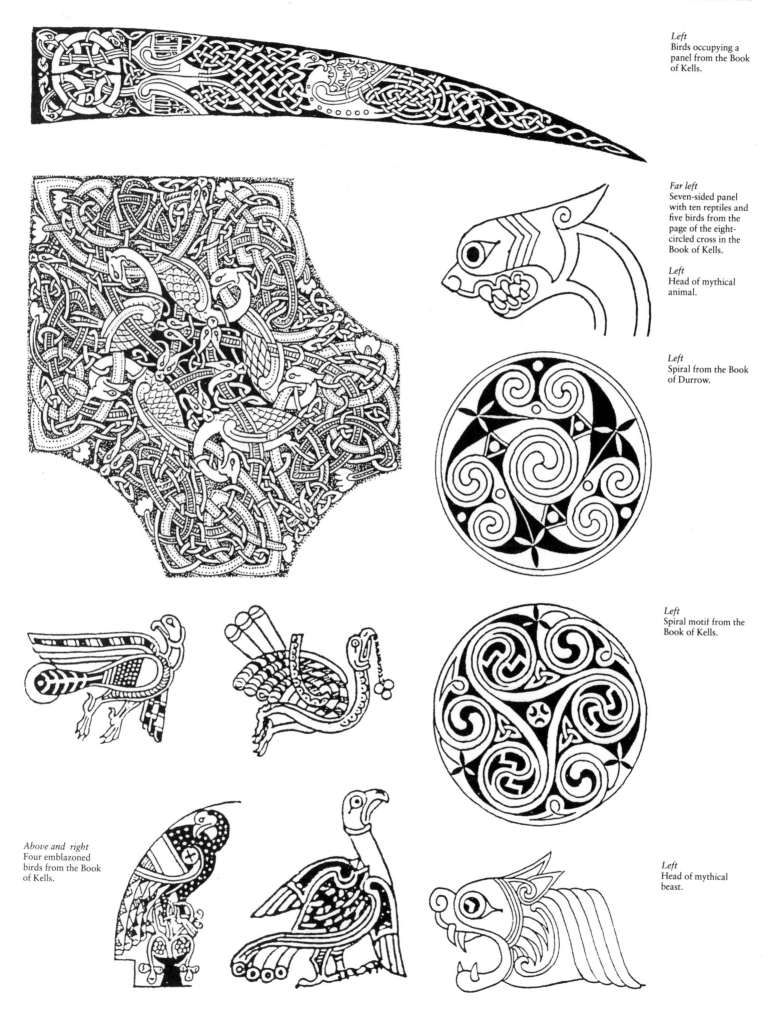

Left
Birds occupying a panel from the Book of Kells.

Far left
Seven-sided panel with ten reptiles and five birds from the page of the eight-circled cross in the Book of Kells.

Left
Head of mythical animal.

Left
Spiral from the Book of Durrow.

Left
Spiral motif from the Book of Kells.

Above and right
Four emblazoned birds from the Book of Kells.

Left
Head of mythical beast.

267

This page
The astonishingly
intricate and patient
work of the Celtic
artists is revealed in
these details of
knotwork, most of
them built up using
only one, single,
interweaving line.

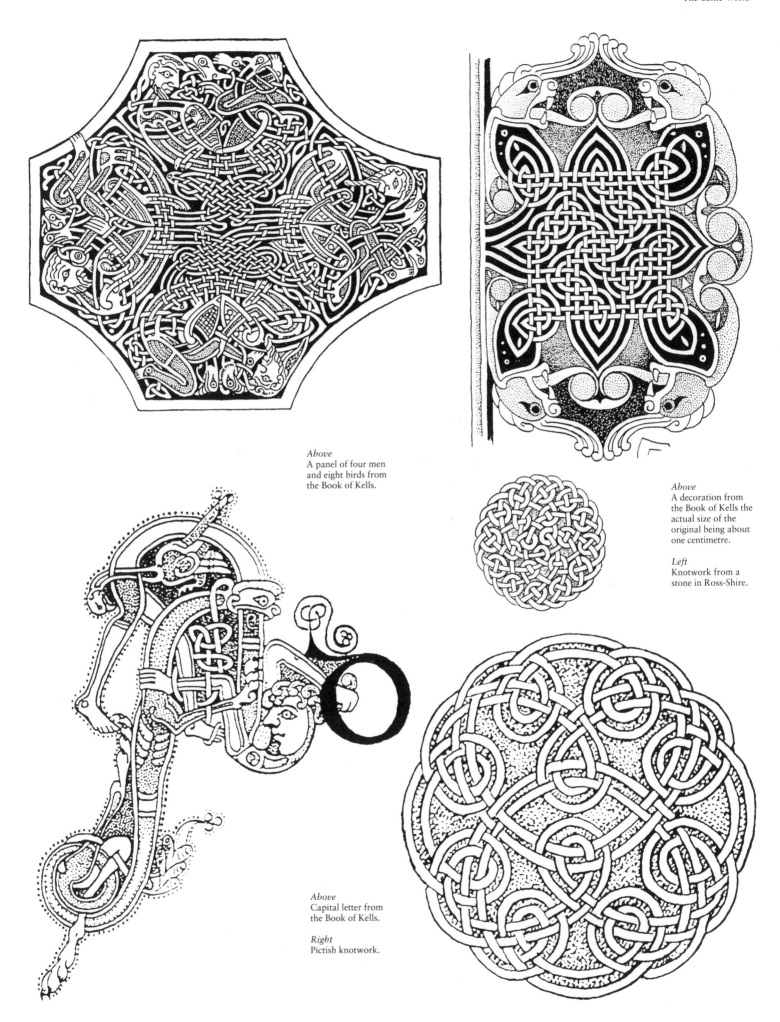

Above
A panel of four men
and eight birds from
the Book of Kells.

Above
A decoration from
the Book of Kells the
actual size of the
original being about
one centimetre.

Left
Knotwork from a
stone in Ross-Shire.

Above
Capital letter from
the Book of Kells.

Right
Pictish knotwork.

269

This page
Varieties of
decorative work
from the pictorial to
the symbolic to the
semi-abstract to the
completely
geometrical.

Right
The base of just one
stroke of the letter
"N" in the Book of
Kells.

Two "A"s from the
Book of Kells.

271

This spread
Capital letters from
the Book of Kells and
the Book of Durrow.

273

This page
Floor tiles, including:
Top left
A hunting design
from Buckingham.

Middle
Rabbit at rest on a
tile from Reading in
Berkshire.

Far right
A hare running.

Right
Butterfly motif from
Derbyshire.

This page
Medieval tiles,
including:
Far left, bottom
A rampant lion on a
tile from Westminster
Abbey.

This spread
Tile designs
employing scenes
from hunting and
jousting with
mythical creatures
and Royal
Personages.

This page
Floor tile designs,
including:
Top
A design utilised in
Sherborne Abbey,
Dorset.

Opposite
Medieval tile designs,
including:
Top
A 13th Century
Fleur-de-Lis design
used in Keynsham
Abbey in Somerset.

279

This spread
Intricate tile decorations utilising heraldic, floral and animal motifs and other insignia.

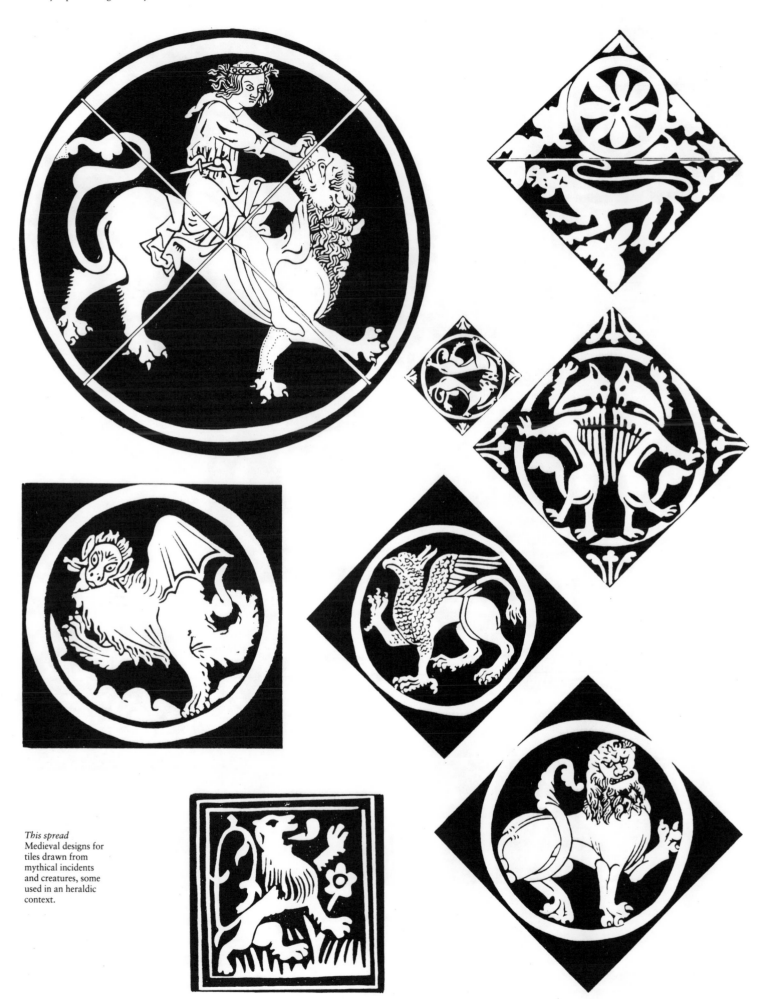

This spread
Medieval designs for
tiles drawn from
mythical incidents
and creatures, some
used in an heraldic
context.

283

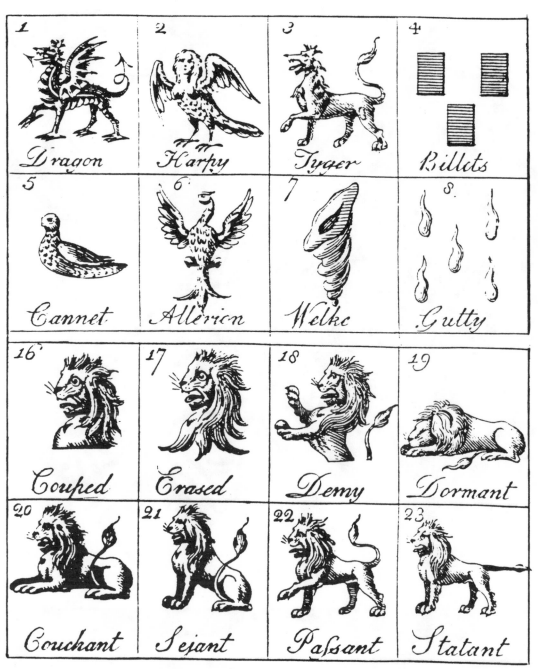

1 Dragon	*2* Harpy	*3* Tyger	*4* Billets
5 Cannet	*6* Allerion	*7* Welke	*8* Gutty
16 Couped	*17* Erased	*18* Demy	*19* Dormant
20 Couchant	*21* Sejant	*22* Passant	*23* Statant

12

Passant Regardant

This page
Various of the positions of the stag and the lion.

Right
Designs of shields
found on Ancient
Greek vases.

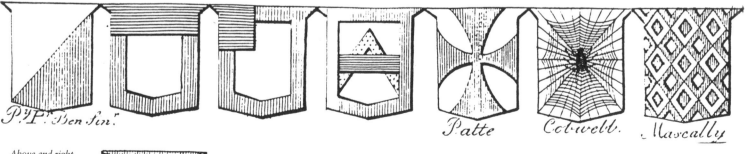

Pᵧ̃Pˡ·Ben.fin⁵.   *Patte*   *Cobwebb.*   *Mascally*

Above and right
Additional details of
the use of the lion
and some heraldic
shields.

Cross of Adelstane

1 Bohemia	*2* Sardinia	*3* Sicily	*4* Holland
5 Orange	*6* Hanover	*7* Palatine	*8* Cologne
9 Waldeck	*10* Mecklenburgh	*11* Genoa	*12* Lorrain
13 Guelderland	*14* Mentz	*15* Catalonia	*16* Parma
17 Guastalla	*18* Baden	*19* Modena	*20* Holstein
21 Hungary	*22* Sweden	*23* Mantua	*24* Valence

This spread
Heraldic crowns.

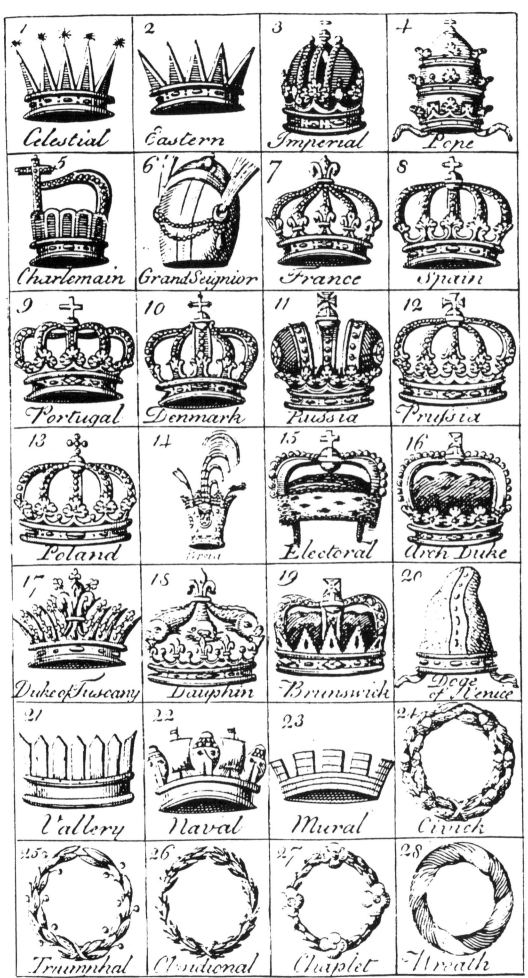

1 Celestial	2 Eastern	3 Imperial	4 Pope
5 Charlemain	6 Grand Seignior	7 France	8 Spain
9 Portugal	10 Denmark	11 Russia	12 Prussia
13 Poland	14 Bruu	15 Electoral	16 Arch Duke
17 Duke of Tuscany	18 Dauphin	19 Brunswick	20 Doge of Venice
21 Vallery	22 Naval	23 Mural	24 Civick
25 Triumphal	26 Obsidional	27 Chaplet	28 Wreath

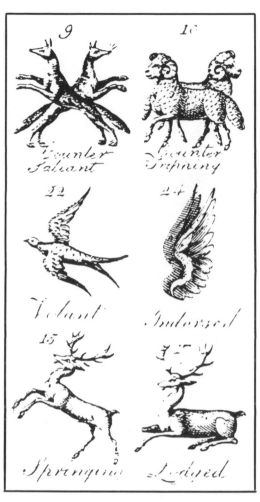

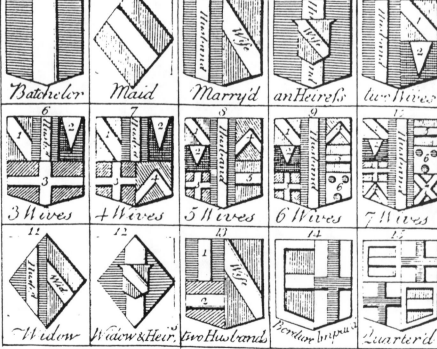

Top
A fabulous beast, called the manticore, comprising a union of a lion, a scorpion and a human head.

Above middle
The crests of Richard I, Henri de Percy and Henri de Laci.

Above
Achievements and Charges.

Top right
Additional positional indications.

Right
Stag configurations.

288

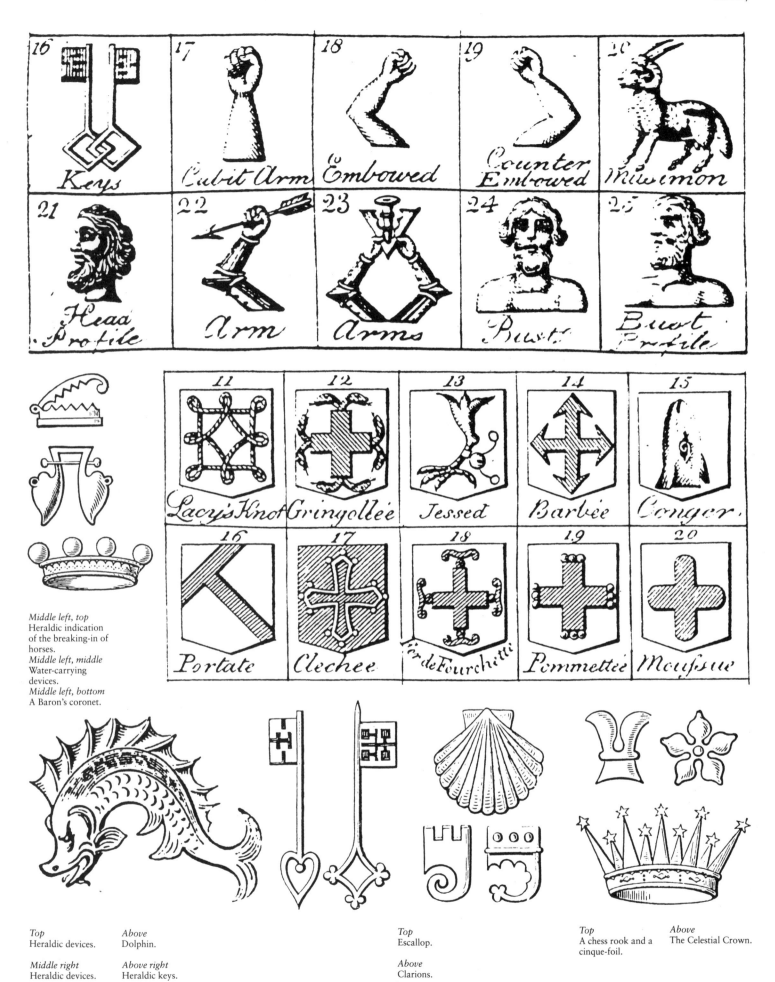

16 Keys
17 Cubit Arm
18 Embowed
19 Counter Embowed
20 Mawemon

21 Head Profile
22 Arm
23 Arms
24 Bust
25 Bust Profile

11 Lacy's Knot
12 Gringollée
13 Jessed
14 Barbée
15 Conger

16 Portate
17 Clechee
18 Fer de Fourchettée
19 Pommettée
20 Moussue

Middle left, top
Heraldic indication of the breaking-in of horses.
Middle left, middle
Water-carrying devices.
Middle left, bottom
A Baron's coronet.

Top
Heraldic devices.

Middle right
Heraldic devices.

Above
Dolphin.

Above right
Heraldic keys.

Top
Escallop.

Above
Clarions.

Top
A chess rook and a cinque-foil.

Above
The Celestial Crown.

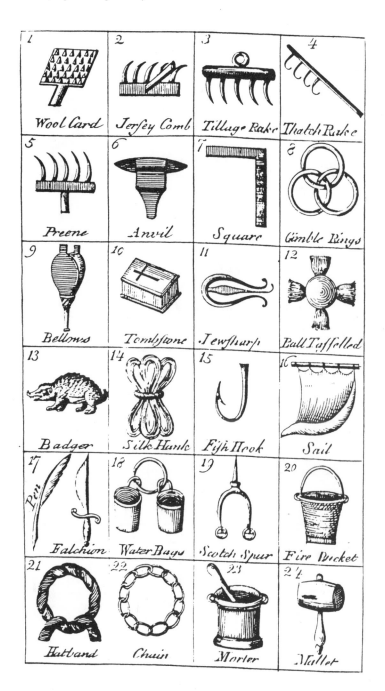

1 Wool Card	2 Jersey Comb	3 Tillage Rake	4 Thatch Rake
5 Preene	6 Anvil	7 Square	8 Gimble Rings
9 Bellows	10 Tombstone	11 Jewsharp	12 Ball Tassdled
13 Badger	14 Silk Hanle	15 Fish Hook	16 Sail
17 Falchion Pen	18 Water Bags	19 Scotch Spur	20 Fire Bucket
21 Hatband	22 Chain	23 Morter	24 Mallet

1 Sagittarius	2 Spinx	3 Sea Horse	4 Mermaid	5 Unicorn
6 Afsis	7 Panther	8 Horse	9 Bear	10 Wolf
11 Elephant	12 Bull	13 Counter Tripping	14 Cock	15 A Signet
16 Owl	17 Cornish Chough	18 Rere mouse	19 Stork	20 Boar
21 Rhinoceros	22 Goat	23 Camel	24 Ostrich	25 Holy Lamb
26 Talbot	27 Caboshed	28 Fretted	29 Sea Lion	30 Leopard
31 Spread Eagle	32 Lobster	33 Attire	34 Lure	35 Hawks Bell

This spread
Heraldic devices.

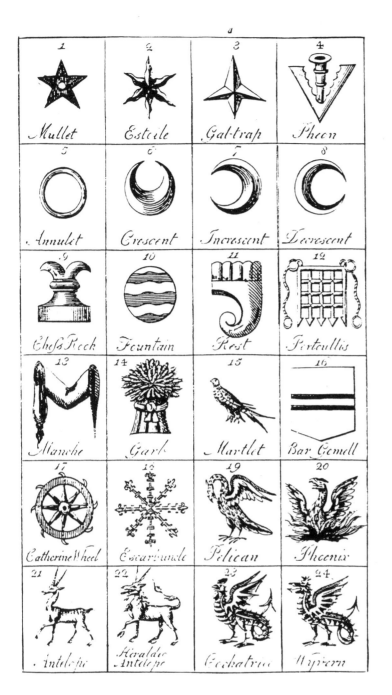

1 Mullet	2 Esteile	3 Gal-trap	4 Pheon
5 Annulet	6 Crescent	7 Increscent	8 Decrescent
9 Chess Rook	10 Fountain	11 Rest	12 Portcullis
13 Manche	14 Garb	15 Martlet	16 Bar Gemell
17 Catherine Wheel	18 Escarbuncle	19 Pelican	20 Phoenix
21 Antelope	22 Heraldic Antelope	23 Cockatrice	24 Wyvern

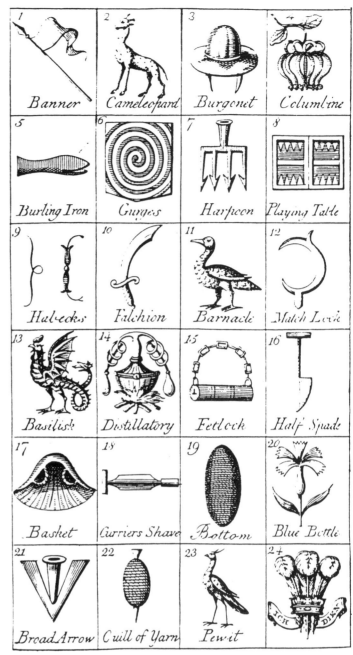

1 Banner	2 Cameleopard	3 Burgonet	4 Columbine
5 Burling Iron	6 Gurges	7 Harpoon	8 Playing Table
9 Hatbecks	10 Falchion	11 Barnacle	12 Match Lock
13 Basilisk	14 Distillatory	15 Fetlock	16 Half Spade
17 Basket	18 Curriers Shave	19 Bottom	20 Blue Bottle
21 Broad Arrow	22 Quill of Yarn	23 Pewet	24

291

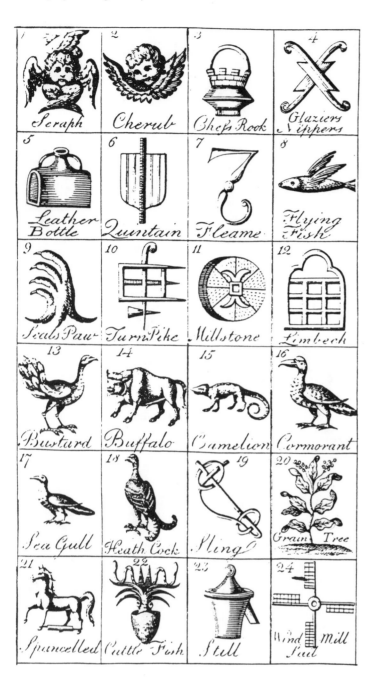

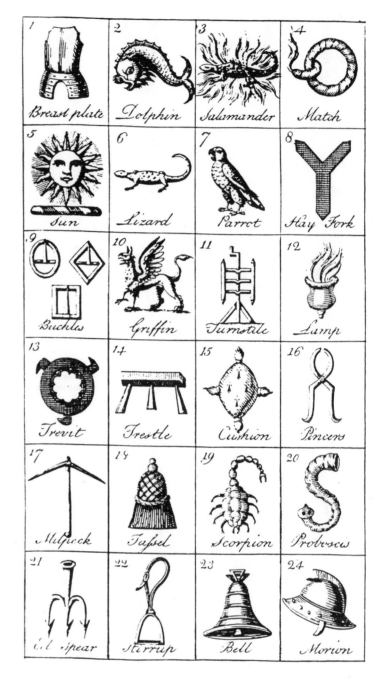

This spread
Heraldic devices.

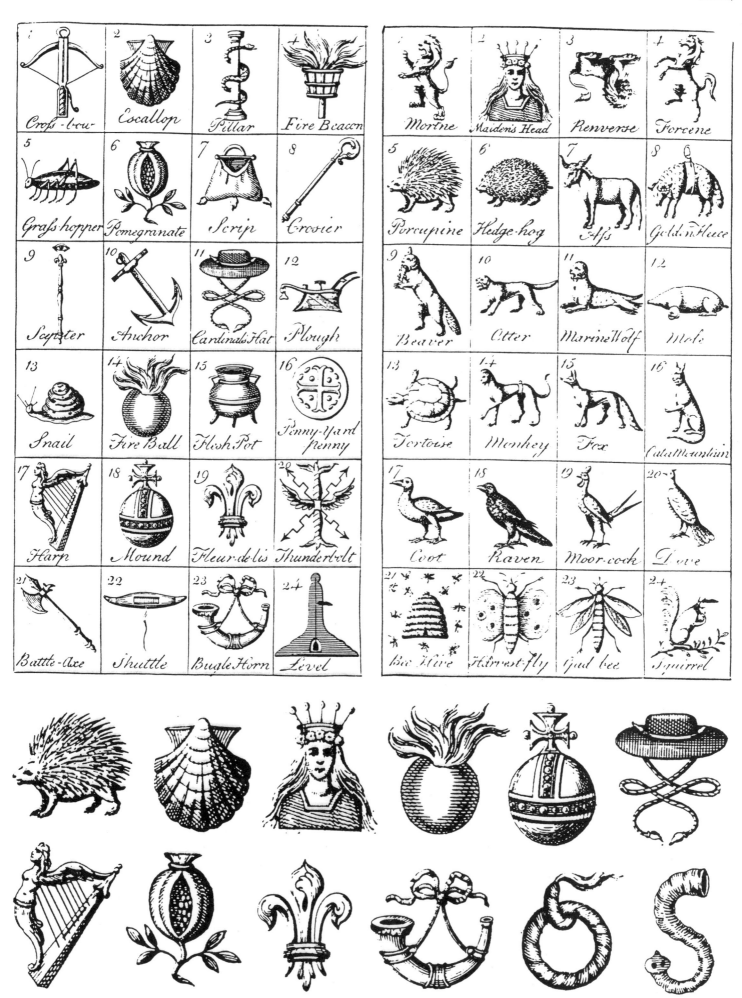

1 Cross-bow	2 Escallop	3 Pillar	4 Fire Beacon
5 Grasshopper	6 Pomegranate	7 Scrip	8 Crosier
9 Scepter	10 Anchor	11 Cardinals Hat	12 Plough
13 Snail	14 Fire Ball	15 Flesh Pot	16 Penny-Yard penny
17 Harp	18 Mound	19 Fleur-de-lis	20 Thunderbolt
21 Battle-Axe	22 Shuttle	23 Bugle Horn	24 Level

1 Mortne	2 Maiden's Head	3 Renverse	4 Forcene
5 Porcupine	6 Hedge-hog	7 Ass	8 Golden Fleece
9 Beaver	10 Otter	11 Marine Wolf	12 Mole
13 Tortoise	14 Monkey	15 Fox	16 Cat a Mountain
17 Coot	18 Raven	19 Moor-cock	20 Dove
21 Bee Hive	22 Harvest-fly	23 Gad-bee	24 Squirrel

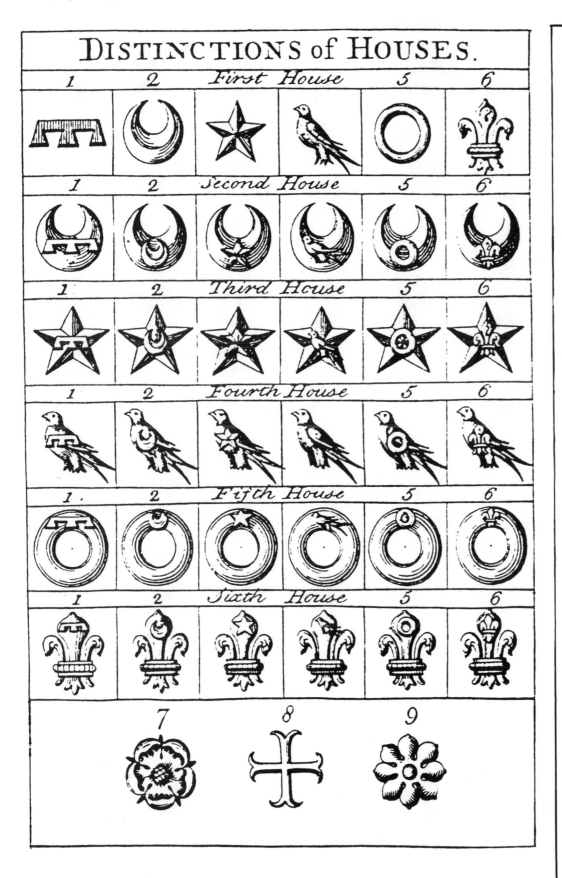

DISTINCTIONS of HOUSES.

1	2	First House		5	6
1	2	Second House		5	6
1	2	Third House		5	6
1	2	Fourth House		5	6
1	2	Fifth House		5	6
1	2	Sixth House		5	6

7	8	9

Above
The marks and accoutrements revealing rank and standing.

Right
Details of the above.

Opposite page
The hatchments delineating family and position and social circumstance.

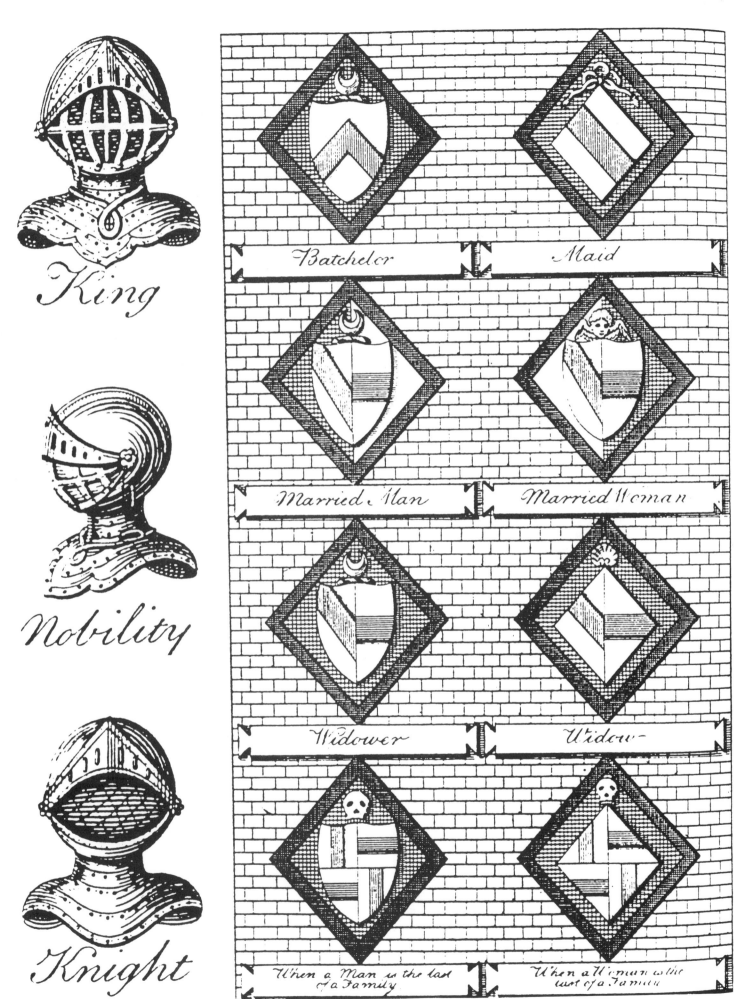

King

Nobility

Knight

Batchelor

Maid

Married Man

Married Woman

Widower

Widow

When a Man is the last of a Family

When a Woman is the last of a Family

Top
The French Imperial
Eagle.

Above
The Arms of John
Rede.

Far right
Detail from the Arms
of William de
Valance.

Near right
Heraldic bird
position.

**Section to right,
above**
Various heraldic
creatures.

DER NEUE
REICHS ADLER

Above
The eagle of the first
German Republic.
Drawn in 1921.

Far left
Two German eagles.

Right
The Winged Lion of
St. Mark.

This spread and the following four pages These last few images, largely decorative motifs and illustrations used in books or as architectural embellishment, are a long way in space and time from the events recorded by Flinders Petrie, whose drawings began this book. But the preoccupations remain the same: geometric form and decorative or symbolic reductions of nature, some, even, suggesting a timelessness unfashionable in our age.

WIENER WERKSTÄTTE
G. M. B. H.
WIEN VII½ NEUSTIFTGASSE 32·34
TELEGR·ADRESSE
WEWE WIEN
TELEFONANRUF
30073·30074
ÖSTERR POSTSPARKASSEN KONTO FUR DEUTSCHLAND
DURCH DIE DEUTSCHE BANK № 149277 WIEN 191

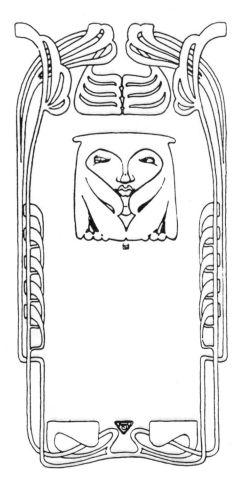

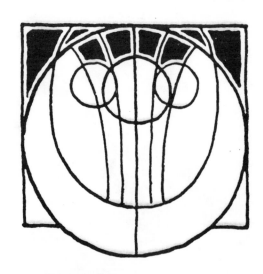

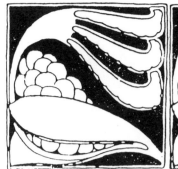

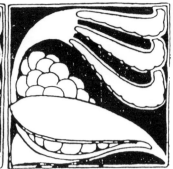

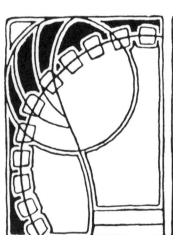

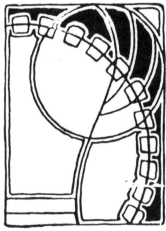

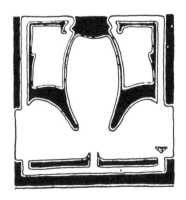

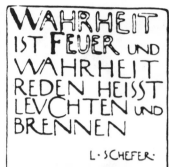

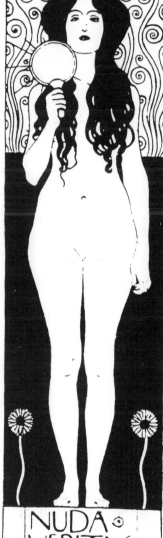

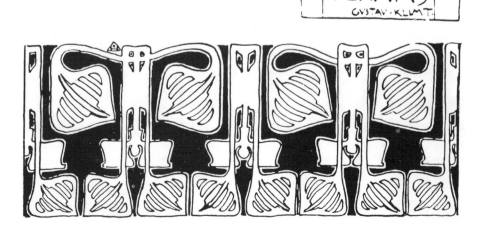

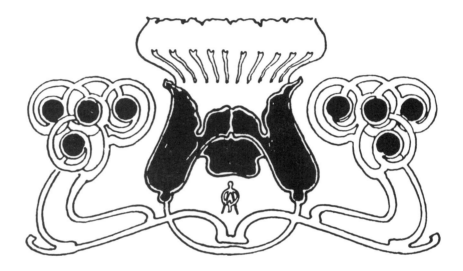

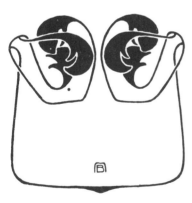

303